SURF
FOOD
THE ULTIMATE SURFERS COOKBOOK

Printed in Singapore by PH productions
1 Ubi Crescent
Singapore, 408563, Singapore

National Library of Australia Cataloguing-in-Publication entry

Author: Young, Nava.
Title: Surf food / Nava Young.
ISBN: 9780646522517 (hbk.)
Subjects: Cookery.
Dewey Number: 641.5

Cover Photos: Simon Williams, Tim McKenna, Tom Servais,
Noah Hamilton, Brian Bielmann, Brenton Geach

SURF
FOOD
THE ULTIMATE SURFERS COOKBOOK
NAVA YOUNG

PANDANUS
PRODUCTIONS
ANGOURIE

Contents

breakfast & smoothies

salads, starters & sides

mains

desserts

swilly.com

Nava Young is a musician, writer and professional surfer. Raised amid a surfing family in Angourie on Australia's East Coast, the ocean plays a major part in her life. In 2008 Nava graduated from SCU earning a Bachelor of Arts in creative writing and international studies. *Surf Food* is her first book.

Introduction

Surf, eat, sleep. It's the ideal combination of activities for most surfers. Spending a large majority of time in the ocean chasing waves makes us a damn hungry bunch of people. As a result we are infamous for our appetites. So just what do the world's best surfers eat? Well, this book answers that very question.

For over two years I have been e-mail stalking the planet's greatest surfers in the hopes of extracting their favourite foods. The recipes contained in this book are as varied and individual as the surfers themselves. You can experience flavours from Japan, Peru, France, America, Hawaii, Brazil, Australia, Mexico and Africa. Accompanying each recipe is a short biography of the achievements and contributions made to the surfing world by these remarkable people.

Surfers are generally passionate individuals and throughout the process of writing this book I have discovered that passion extends very much to the kitchen. From Mickey Dora's ceaseless hunt around provincial France in search of the perfect truffle to Bob McTavish's quest for the ideal chilli relleno. One thing is for certain; we take our food seriously and love to seek out amazing nosh with the same relish as a perfect right-hander.

I personally love to cook, but become irritated when a recipe, which professes to be simple, takes me forever to prepare. Being a non master-chef, food usually ends up on the walls and the finished product barely resembles the glossy picture accompanying the recipe. Don't worry, my friends, this book is NOT like that! Most of the recipes are simple to make and I have tested them all with my average culinary skills. My family and friends, a large majority of whom are surfers, have been excellent taste testers and every single recipe contained in this book has been given the thumbs up by at least a couple of my crew. Importantly, lots of the foods in this book can be made in minutes.

As wave riders and human beings I feel we all have a responsibility to look after each other and this wonderful world we live in. The surfers in this book share that sentiment. Therefore 10% of all profits are being donated to surfing charities.

There are numerous comparisons between a great meal and an excellent wave, both are experienced only for a short time, both nourish and can be shared with friends and family. I wish you all an abundance of fantastic waves and fabulous food. Hopefully this book helps you on your journey.

breakfasts & smoothies

Mike Doyle

mikedoyle.com

Mike Doyle is surfing's renaissance man. An artist, entrepreneur, inventor and waterman, Mike is considered a surfing icon.

Doyle was thirteen when he fell in love with surfing at Manhattan Beach. Just five years later he was one of America's's best surfers. With his classic Californian good looks, athletic build and outgoing personality, Doyle became one of the eras most charismatic characters. His wins at the Makaha International and the 1969 Duke Invitational, cemented his status as one of the world's most talented surfers.

Mike took to the ocean on various forms of equipment and had competitive success as both a tandem surfer and paddleboard racer. He influenced a generation of surfers with his panache both in and out of the water.

Always the innovator, Doyle manufactured the first surfboard specific wax and is responsible for the popular soft surfboard. In 1970 he invented the single ski, a predecessor of today's snowboard.

In recent decades Doyle has expressed his artistic side from his Baja home. His colorful paintings have enjoyed commercial and critical success. Doyle has also released his autobiography, *Morning Glass*, which chronicles his infamous adventures. An inductee to the Surfing Hall of Fame, Mike spends his time snowboarding, painting and of course surfing.

larry castruita

Huevos Mexicanos

This classic Mexican breakfast serves 2 and is perfect after an early morning surf. Can be served with rice for a heartier meal.

ingredients

4 eggs

½ bunch of coriander/cilantro

1 tomato

1 capsicum/bell pepper

1 small onion

1 can of refried or black beans

6 corn tortillas

Hot sauce, salt and pepper to taste

1 tablespoon of olive oil

method

- Wrap corn tortillas in foil and heat in oven until warm.
- Chop tomato, capsicum and onion into bite sized pieces.
- Heat a large pan/skillet to medium. Add oil and fry onions for 5 minutes.
- Add capsicum and tomato. Fry until tender.
- Whisk eggs in a separate bowl.
- Chop coriander finely and fold through eggs.
- Pour egg mixture into frying pan and cook until set, stirring gently.
- Season with hot sauce, salt and pepper.
- Heat beans and serve immediately with eggs and warm tortillas.

Lisa Andersen

Lisa Andersen is a world champion, mother and inspiration to women all over the globe. In the 1990s Lisa combined her beauty and supernatural talent to revolutionise women's surfing and win four Association of Surfing Professionals (ASP) World Titles.

Andersen grew up in Ormond Beach, Florida, where she was one of a few girls who surfed. At sixteen she ran away from home leaving a note saying she was going to become a world champion surfer. Despite solid performances on tour and numerous wins, a world title remained elusive. It would take the birth of her daughter, Erica, in 1993 to give Andersen the focus needed to reach the pinnacle of her sport. Lisa won world titles in 1994, '95, '96 and '97, after which a chronic back injury forced her into early retirement.

Lisa has been a cover girl for numerous sports magazines and been named one of the twenty five most influential surfers of all time. She runs surf camps, makes celebrity appearances in films, has a video game character, a star on the Surfing Walk of Fame and a day job with long-time sponsor, Roxy.

Despite her success Lisa remains humble, relishing her role as a mum of two and a spokesperson for female surfers everywhere. Banana pancakes are one of Lisa's favourite post-surf foods.

Banana Pancakes

This yummy breakfast recipe serves 2.

ingredients

1 cup of plain flour

1 tablespoon of white sugar

2 teaspoons of baking powder

¼ teaspoon of salt

1 egg

1 cup of milk

1 teaspoon of vanilla essence

1 tablespoon of vegetable oil

2 ripe bananas

Maple syrup to serve

method

- In a large bowl combine flour, white sugar, baking powder and salt.
- Mash bananas and set aside.
- In a separate bowl, lightly beat egg then mix with milk, vegetable oil and bananas.
- Stir flour mixture into banana mixture.
- Heat frying pan to medium.
- Lightly grease with butter then use a ladle to scoop batter into pan.
- Cook until pancakes are golden brown on both sides.
- Serve immediately with butter and maple syrup.
- Garnish with extra banana slices if desired.

Sam Bleakley

russ pierre

Sam Bleakley is a champion surfer who has numerous British and European Titles to his credit. The multi talented Bleakley graduated from Cambridge University and has since combined his surfing career with freelance journalism.

Sam's extensive travels have seen him venture far from his Cornish home and broaden the boundaries of surf exploration. He has been one of the first people photographed surfing in several countries such as South Korea, Haiti and Kenya.

Thanks to his father introducing him to the surfing lifestyle at a young age, the ocean has always played a major part in Sam's life. The motivation provided by his family and former British champion, Roger Mansfield, saw Sam accomplish the amazing feat of winning the English, British and European Longboard Surfing titles in the same year.

Today Sam still lives in his hometown of Sennen Cove, Cornwall with his wife Sandy and daughter Lola. He continues to write, compete and travel while remaining inspired by the ocean and those around him. His first book, a collection of surf stories chronicling his many adventures will be released in the near future.

russ pierre

Fruit Salad with Honey Spiced Yogurt

gutter photos

This nutritious breakfast serves 4. Note that fruit can be varied seasonally or to your tastes.

ingredients

Spiced Honey Yoghurt

2 cups of plain Greek yoghurt

3 tablespoons of honey

1 teaspoon of vanilla essence

½ teaspoon of cinnamon

Pinch of dried mixed spice

Fruit Salad

1 pear

1 mango

1 banana

1 nectarine or peach

½ cup of blueberries

½ cup of strawberries

½ cup of raspberries

method

Spiced Honey Yogurt

• Mix yoghurt, honey, vanilla, mixed spice and cinnamon in a medium bowl.
• Cover and place in fridge.

Fruit Salad

• Cut all fruit into bite sized pieces and combine in a large bowl.
• Add banana last as it browns if left out too long.
• Toss fruit and serve with yoghurt.
• Additionally you may sprinkle coconut or drizzle fresh passion fruit to serve.

Barton Lynch

courtesy barton lynch

Barton Lynch (BL) has been a principal figure in Australian surfing for almost thirty years. His natural ability combined with competitive savvy saw Lynch through a remarkable professional career that spanned fifteen years, resulting in seventeen WCT victories and a superb World Title win in 1988.

Barton grew up surfing in Sydney's Northern Beaches, after triumphant success as a junior, he turned pro in 1983. Lynch's stunning fairytale win in 1988 remains one of the most exciting World Title finishes in surfing's history. On the last day of the season's final event, Lynch was in third place for the crown. Remarkably his rivals were eliminated early and Barton went on to win both the contest and the title.

In 1998, after a long and illustrious career, Lynch retired from competition. Both intelligent and socially aware, Barton has lent his name to numerous charities and causes. Lynch's outgoing personality has also made him one of surfing's most visible media characters.

Today Barton still lives in Sydney with his daughter where he runs his own consultancy firm called The Surfers Group (bartonlynch.com). BL uses his extensive experience to coach, train and mentor many aspiring champions. He gives back to surfing by running his own under 14s' surf contest, BL's Blast Off.

wheresharro.com

Aussie Bacon & Poached Eggs

twaddlebean

This is a breakfast staple with an Aussie twist! Serves 2.

ingredients

2 fresh room temperature free range eggs

4 slices of good quality bacon

1 tablespoon of white vinegar

4 slices of bread

Butter

Vegemite or promite

method

- Fill a large non stick frying pan or saucepan with about 8cm (3 inches) of water.
- Cover water with lid and place on high heat.
- Crack eggs into 2 separate small bowls or cups.
- When water boils, remove lid and add vinegar and a pinch of salt.
- Place the rim of each cup about 1cm (½ inch) below the water and let the egg flow out.
- Repeat for each egg.
- Immediately turn off heat and reapply lid. Set a timer for exactly 3 minutes.
- While the eggs are cooking, heat non-stick pan to medium temperature.
- Add the slices of bacon and cook for a few minutes until crisp.
- Constantly turn bacon while cooking.
- Toast bread. Then spread with butter and vegemite/promite to taste.
- When timer goes off, lift each egg out of the water with a spoon.
- Place egg on toast, top with bacon and another slice of toast.

Nat Young

Nat Young is one of the most influential surfers of the twentieth century. A five time World Champion and key contributor to both the shortboard revolution and the longboarding renaissance, Young is a surfing legend.

Born Robert Young in 1947, he earned the nickname "Gnat" for being the smallest grommet at his Collaroy Beach home. The nickname became "Nat" when he shot to six feet, two inches and won the Open Men's National Title at sixteen.

In 1966 Young bought his power surfing to the World Championships in California. He dominated, winning convincingly and ushering in a new era of surfing. Despite being the foremost competitor of the period, Nat quit competition in 1970 and got back to nature in Byron Bay. He re-entered the world of competition in the '80s, this time riding longboards. He was successful to say the least, winning a staggering four Longboard World Titles.

Young has been a fashion model, successful entrepreneur and philanthropist. He has written five books and made two films based around his love of surfing. Today Young still endeavors to "make it a beautiful life". The father of four, divides his time between surfing Angourie, working on his farm and snowboarding in Sun Valley, Idaho.

swilly.com

Home-made Toasted Muesli

gutter.photos

Nat believes that the first meal of the day is the most important. His Californian friend Marsha bought this recipe to Australia in the '60s, when Muesli was unknown.

ingredients

5 tablespoons of olive oil

7 tablespoons of honey

250g (9 oz) of almond kernels and flakes

250g (9 oz) of pecan halves and pieces

200g (7 oz) of sunflower kernels

3 cups of rolled oats

2 cups of shredded coconut (not desiccated)

method

- Preheat oven to 150°C (300°F).
- In a large, thick based oven-proof baking dish, heat olive oil and honey on stove top to medium heat.
- Add all nuts and seeds. Stir continuously over heat until coated (approximately 2 minutes).
- Add oats and cook stirring constantly for a further 2 minutes.
- Add coconut and stir. Remove from stove stop.
- Place baking dish in oven and cook for 30 minutes. Every 3 minutes remove dish from oven and stir. This ensures that the muesli is toasted evenly. It's a bit of a hassle but is well worth it!
- Cool and store in an airtight container. Serve with yoghurt and fresh fruit.

Bethany Hamilton

Bethany Hamilton is one of the world's most inspirational people. The talented teenager survived a brutal shark attack, then overcame immense odds to not only surf again, but compete at an elite level.

Born in the Hawaiian paradise of Kauai, Bethany was introduced to surfing as a toddler. Family support combined with natural ability saw Bethany climb the ranks of amateur competition and attract the attention of international sponsors. In summer 2003 Bethany placed second in the National Scholastic Surfing Association (NSSA) nationals, her dream of becoming a professional surfer was within reach.

On October 31st 2003 Bethany's life changed forever when she was attacked by a four meter tiger shark, leaving her with a severed left arm. Amazingly less than one month later Bethany was surfing again. Remarkably in 2005 she won the NSSA national championship.

Today Bethany is successfully climbing the ranks of the World Qualifying Series (WQS) with many impressive results. She combines her surfing with charity work and is an ambassador for World Vision. Out of the water Bethany keeps busy representing her many sponsors, writing books and making motivational speeches. The winner of numerous awards, including an ESPY for Best Comeback, she is a positive role model for young women everywhere.

Acai Carob Mint Shake

bethanyhamilton.com

As healthy eating is part of Bethany's training regime, she has chosen to include this luscious smoothie recipe. Sponsored by Sambazon Acai, Bethany makes this shake when her sweet tooth kicks in!

ingredients

2 Sambazon Acai smoothie packs
1-2 frozen bananas
⅓ cup of carob powder
Dash of cinnamon
1½ cups of almond milk

Handful of fresh mint leaves or 2-3 drops of mint extract
1 tablespoon of spirulina powder
3-5 tablespoons of hemp protein

method

• Place all ingredients in blender and mix until smooth.
• Serve in a chilled glass and garnish with mint leaves.

Kelly Slater

andrew shield

Kelly Slater is the best competitive surfer in history. For twenty years his astonishing talent has changed the way surfers approach waves. With an extraordinary nine ASP World Titles, forty-one World Circuit Tour wins and two X-Games Gold Medals to his credit, Kelly is surfing's superstar.

Born in Coco Beach Florida, Kelly grew up surfing with his brothers. By age eleven he was dominating amateur competitions. He turned pro at eighteen and along with friends ushered in surfing's new school.

ASP rookie of the year in 1991, Kelly won his first world title in 1992. Since then he has claimed eight more and holds the distinction of being both the youngest and oldest world champion. Aside from his competitive accomplishments, Kelly's explosive free surfing, spontaneous maneuvers, style and professionalism continue to change the surfer archetype.

Slater's extraordinary athletic abilities have garnered him recognition beyond the surfing world. He has starred in TV shows and even has his own video game. Humble despite the intense amount of attention, Kelly supports numerous charities and gives back to surfing.

swilly.com

Avocado Smoothie

This is a quick vegan smoothie recipe, which is simple to make and extremely nutritious.

ingredients
1 avocado
1¼ cups of distilled water
Pinch of Himalayan sea salt
1 teaspoon of vanilla extract/essence
Agave syrup/nectar to taste

method
• Mix all ingredients together in blender until smooth.
• Serve in a chilled glass over ice.

Jennifer Smith

Jen Smith is undoubtedly one of the best female longboard surfers in the world. So far this young talent has had a stellar career which has included numerous contest wins, a North American Title and most notably the 2007 and 2009 ASP World Titles.

Born in San Diego California, Jen was raised on the beach. Her father, Pablo Smith, has worked in the surf and skate industry for over thirty years. With roots such as these it is no wonder that Jen was naturally drawn to surfing.

At sixteen Jen decided that longboarding was the right fit for her and hasn't looked back since. Her smooth style and relaxed attitude, combined with the backing of surfing giant Roxy, have made Jen one of longboarding's most recognisable faces.

Although most of Smith's time is spent travelling the globe for contests and photo shoots, when she is home she enjoys spending time with her family and friends, cooking and hanging out with her boxer dog, Colin. Jen makes this delicious smoothie for breakfast or as a light pre surf snack.

tim mckenna

tim mckenna

Blueberry Almond Smoothie

Serves 1.

ingredients

1 banana

120-160g (4-6 oz) of blueberries

Soy milk

1 heaped tablespoon of almond butter

Small handful of raisins (optional)

4 ice cubes

method

• Place blueberries in a large glass and add enough soy milk to just cover the blueberries.

• Add this to the blender along with banana, ice, almond butter and raisins.

• Mix all ingredients together until liquefied.

• Serve, drink and go surfing.

salads, starters and sides

Jim Banks

tom servais

Jim Banks is a surfboard shaper, musician and world-class tube rider. Throughout the late '70s and '80s, Jim became known for taking on the world's most dangerous waves, often solo, and leaving the competitive circuit to pursue an alternate lifestyle.

Growing up on Sydney's Cronulla Beach, it seemed inevitable that Jim would become a surfer. At ten years old Banks rode his first wave. Seven years later he found himself surfing professionally and shaping at the iconic Gordon and Smith surfboard factory. A solo trip to Bali in 1977 was a life changing event for Jim, establishing his passion for flawless barrels and distant locations.

Jim launched himself on the pro tour in 1978 on a self shaped board. Three years later after winning the 1981 Om Bali Pro in the flawless waves of Uluwatu, Jim walked away from the craziness of the competitive scene to resume his passion for free surfing.

These days, Jim is still roaming the planet seeking out perfect waves in remote regions. When in Australia, he bases himself just south of Byron Bay where he leads the occasional health retreat and self-awareness workshop. Recently he has begun building guitars and amplifiers for musicians such as The Beautiful Girls and Ash Grunwald.

tim mckenna

Organic Chicken Feta Salad

twadlebean

This is a perfect recipe to make when you have leftover cooked chicken. Alternately you can buy a barbequed chicken or start from scratch and roast your own. If desired substitute the chicken with tofu, tempeh, chorizo or fish. Recipe serves 4.

ingredients

500g (1.1 lb) of cooked chicken

300g (10.5 oz) of feta cheese

½ cup of mung bean sprouts

½ cup of mixed sprouts

2 tomatoes

1 capsicum/bell pepper

1 medium sized cucumber

1 cup of fresh spinach

1 cup of cabbage

1 lime

Olive oil to taste

Salt and pepper

¼ cup of lightly toasted pumpkin seeds for a bit more crunch (optional)

method

• Dice tomatos, capsicum and cucumber. Shred spinach and cabbage.
• Combine in a large salad bowl with sprouts.
• Squeeze in lime juice and toss.
• Dice chicken and feta. Add to salad.
• Toss with a generous amount of extra virgin olive oil.
• Season with salt and pepper.
• Serve.

Rochelle Ballard

Rochelle Ballard is generally considered one of the best female tube riders ever. Rochelle pushed the envelope of women's surfing conquering some of the most powerful waves in the world. During the '90s Ballard greatly contributed to changing the expectations of what females could accomplish in the ocean.

Both beautiful and easygoing, the five feet, one inch tall Ballard is regarded as the first woman to master consistent tube riding. She is a veteran competitive surfer with a career spanning over two decades. As female surfing became increasingly high-performance, Ballard led the charge into bigger and better waves. Notably Ballard was a stunt double for *Blue Crush*, the multimillion-dollar Universal Pictures blockbuster.

Rochelle is one of the most popular female surfers of all time. She has won many accolades within the industry and appeared in countless magazines, books and movies. A successful multi-tasker Rochelle has contributed to many publications and co-founded a lobbying group, all while running surf camps and producing yoga and surf films.

Rochelle leads an active lifestyle in Hawaii where she works on her many projects. Not surprisingly her recipe is the healthy and delicious Crazy Love Salad.

Crazy Love Salad

rochelleballard.com

This salad is sweet and juicy. It can be altered to your tastes and is best made with the freshest veggies possible. Serves 4.

ingredients

100g (3.5 oz) of baby spinach

100g (3.5 oz) of mixed greens

1 carrot

1 beetroot

1 zucchini

50g (2 oz) of spouts

1 floret of broccoli

Basil, coriander/cilantro and sea salt to taste

Juice of one whole lemon

Dressing

Olive oil

Balsamic vinegar

Apple cider vinegar

Brags amino acids

method

- Grate carrot, beetroot and zucchini.
- Roughly chop broccoli, basil and coriander.
- Toss all ingredients together in large bowl.

Dressing

- Combine ingredients in a separate bowl and mix together. This dressing is based on personal preference and should be experimented with.
- Pour dressing over salad, toss and serve.

John Peck

tom servais

John Peck is famous throughout the surfing world for his exceptional wave riding ability, uncanny timing and spiritual lifestyle.

Peck began surfing in Coronado, California but improved drastically after moving to Waikiki, Hawaii. John became famous on New Years Day 1963 when he paddled out at epic Pipeline on Oahu's North shore, becoming one of the first natural footers to ride deep backside within Pipelines' famous barrels.

For the past thirty years Peck has been the envy of surfers everywhere for his amazing, almost psychic, ability to predict where the waves will be best on any given swell. It is almost guaranteed that if you follow Peck, you are bound to get the optimum conditions.

Today Peck resides in Southern California. He usually surfs daily going wherever the swell takes him. A yoga master, John lives an organic vegan lifestyle. He draws on his extensive life experience to inspire and mentor many younger surfers while simultaneously completing his much anticipated autobiography. After fifty years of surfing he is still stoked and smiling after every ride.

Peck's Mother Bettye has owned Coronado's landmark hotel The Villa Capri for over 40 years. In tribute to her John has named his recipe the Villa Capri Surfer Salad.

tom servais

Villa Capri Surfer Salad

twaddlebean

Recipe serves 4-6. It is best made with as many organic ingredients as possible.

ingredients

150g (5 oz) of baby greens

2 tomatoes

2 stalks of celery

2 tablespoons of tahini

1 apple

1 avocado

⅓ cup of crumbled pecans

½ cup of sunflower seeds

⅓ cup of crumbled walnuts

Bee pollen, cayenne pepper and
Himalayan salt to taste

2 cups of cooked brown rice or quinoa (note
this ingredient can be left out if you want a
lighter meal)

Dressing

2 tablespoons of tahini

1 tablespoon of apple cider vinegar

2 tablespoons of honey

¼ cup of olive oil

method

- Chop tomatoes, apple and avocado into bite sized pieces.
- Place rice or quinoa in the bottom of a large salad bowl.
- Top with baby greens, tomatoes, apple, avocado, nuts, seeds and pollen.
- Chop celery into strips and fill with tahini. Arrange on top of other ingredients.
- Sprinkle with salt and pepper to taste.
- *Dressing:* In a separate bowl mix all ingredients with a fork until combined.
- Pour dressing over salad. Toss and serve.

Sage Erickson

courtesy sage erickson

Sage Erickson is one of surfing's rising stars. At just eighteen the multitalented Erickson has won the ultra competitive NSSA regional championships seven times.

Sage was born on December 28th 1990, in Ojai California. However it was when her family moved to the surfing mecca of Oahu, Hawaii, that Sage discovered her love of the ocean. Erickson rode her first wave at Sunset Beach at the age of ten and has been a surfer ever since. When the family moved back to California she translated what she had learned in the tropics to the perfect point breaks of Ventura and Santa Barbara.

Since then, Sage has taken the competitive surfing world by storm winning numerous contests and gaining a reputation as one of America's most promising juniors. Undoubtedly Erickson has the ability to compete with the best female surfers in the world.

She is currently attempting to join the ranks of the elite World Circuit Tour by competing on the grueling WQS. With the support of her family and sponsors the possibilities seem boundless for Sage.

courtesy sage erickson

Chinese Chicken Salad

twaddlebean

This tasty salad has just the right amount of crunch. To turn this salad into a delicious vegetarian dish simply substitute tofu for chicken. Serves 4-6.

ingredients

500g (1.1 lb) of boneless chicken breasts

400g (14 oz) of Cos or romaine lettuce

2 carrots

1 bunch of shallots/scallions

1 bunch of coriander/cilantro

16 wonton sheets or 1 cup of crispy

chow mein noodles

Dressing

6 tablespoons of hoi sin sauce

6 tablespoons of rice wine vinegar

4 tablespoons of peanut butter

4 teaspoons of brown sugar

2 tablespoons of sesame oil

1 teaspoon of hot chilli paste

2 teaspoons of grated fresh ginger

method

- *Dressing:* Mix all dressing ingredients together. Set aside.
- Cut chicken into bite sized pieces.
- Marinate chicken in half the dressing. Refrigerate for a few hours. Please note that if you are rushed for time you don't have to marinate, but it does taste better if you do.
- Sauté chicken in a large frying pan until cooked through.
- Preheat oven to 180°C (350°F). Spray baking tray with non-stick oil and arrange torn wontons/noodles into a single layer. Bake for 20 minutes till golden brown.
- Wash and shred lettuce. Grate carrot. Finely chop shallots and coriander.
- In a large salad bowl mix together lettuce, carrots, shallots, coriander, chicken and noodles/wontons. Toss with remaining dressing and serve.

Josh Constable

joshconstable.com

Josh Constable is a first class surfer. The 2006 ASP Longboard World Champion made history in 2009 by becoming the first ever Australian Stand Up Paddle National Champion.

Josh grew up among the fabled point breaks of Noosa. Introduced to the water by his Dad, Josh dreamt of becoming a professional surfer. Noosa's perfect rights provided Constable with the ideal environment to make his dream a reality. After extensive success as a junior he turned pro at fifteen.

Constable has enjoyed many great results, including winning the Australian National Longboard Title an incredible five times. A US Open finalist, Josh has won the prestigious Noosa Festival of Surfing on multiple occasions and has been named one of the sports most influential surfers by Longboard Magazine.

Not content to solely longboard, Constable rides anything that will enhance his enjoyment of the ocean. Shortboards, longboards, logs and stand up paddles are all in Josh's quiver. As a result he rips on any surf craft.

Josh resides on the Sunshine coast with his wife Anna, a former World Tandem Champion, and their sons Jet and Jive.

peter artchison

Cheesy Kabana and Bacon Soup

Serves 4-6.

ingredients

2 tablespoons of olive oil

1 white onion

3 cloves of garlic

2 x kabana/cabanossi sausages

3 rashers of bacon, rind removed

1 carrot

½ a red onion

1 litre (2 pints) of chicken stock

1x 420g (14 oz) can of creamed corn

300ml (10 oz) thickened cream at room temp.

Substitute light evaporated milk if desired

1 potato

4 slices of processed cheese

Salt & pepper to taste

Grated cheese, tobasco sauce and chilli

flakes to garnish

method

• Peel and dice potato, white onion and carrot. Crush garlic and slice cheese squares.

• In a large pot, heat oil to medium, add onion and garlic. Cook until transparent.

• Add kabana and bacon. Cook until brown and crispy. It's ok if bits stick to the bottom.

• Add carrot and red onion. Continue cooking for 2 minutes.

• Add chicken stock and as much water as needed to cover mixture.

• Bring to boil and scrape bottom to loosen yummy bits. Turn heat down to low setting.

• Add creamed corn and then cream (add in this order otherwise the cream will curdle).

• Bring back up to boil. Add potato and sliced cheese then season with salt and pepper.

• Cover and simmer for 30 minutes until potato is soft.

• To serve garnish with grated cheese, tobasco and chilli flakes.

Dane Reynolds

swilly.com

Dane Reynolds is a surfing phenomenon. Incredibly talented, yet humble despite being possibly the best free surfer in the world. He combines mind-blowing manoeuvres with a silk smooth style.

Dane honed his talent on the waves surrounding his Ventura, California home. At sixteen he made it to the finals of the super competitive NSSA nationals, where the surfing world first noticed his potential.

After an impressive amateur career Reynolds deviated from the norm and instead of slogging it out on the WQS made his signature film the aptly titled *First Chapter*. The film went on to win several accolades including the Best Male Performance and Video of the Year at the 2006 Surfer Poll and Surf Video Awards.

Dane qualified for the WCT in 2007. It is refreshing that Dane stays true to himself in a sport which rewards competitiveness and at times cut throat tactics. Reynolds refuses to alter his surfing to fit a limited criteria, never compromising his astounding skill for points, titles or ratings. His fan base grows daily.

Reynolds is at the forefront of innovative progressive surfing creating aerial maneuvers that don't have names and need to be viewed in slow motion to be understood. Dane is surfing's future and we can't wait to see what happens next.

swilly.com

Tortilla Soup

Recipe serves 2.

ingredients

1 cup plus 1 tablespoon of oil
(grapeseed, olive or vegetable oil is fine)
3 corn tortillas
2 cloves of garlic
500g (1.1 lb) jar of salsa. Can range from
medium to hot depending on preference.

2 cups of chicken broth/stock
1½ cups of shredded cooked chicken
1 avocado
1 lime
¾ cup of grated cheese
1 bunch of coriander/cilantro

method

• Cut tortillas into small strips.
• Place 1 cup of oil in small saucepan on high heat. Fry tortilla strips in hot oil until they are crisp and golden brown. Carefully remove from oil and drain on paper towels. Set aside.
• Finely chop garlic, avocado and coriander.
• Place 1 tablespoon of oil in saucepan on medium heat. Add garlic and sauté for 2-3 minutes. Add salsa. Stir.
• Add the chicken stock/broth and chicken. Let this simmer slowly for 7-10 minutes.
• Just before serving add half the tortilla strips to soup.
• In a small bowl mix together onion, avocado, coriander and the juice of one lime.
• Serve soup in bowls.
• Top with grated cheese, avocado mixture and the remaining tortilla strips.

Donald Takayama

kevin kinnear

Donald Takayama is without a doubt one of the world's greatest surfboard shapers. Both artist and craftsman, Takayama has built a life around his love of the ocean.

Born in the tropical paradise of Hawaii, Donald began surfing at seven and started shaping shortly thereafter. In 1957 at just twelve years of age Takayama bought a plane ticket to Los Angeles and started working among several of California's elite shapers. He made boards for the top pro's and designed some of the most innovative and sought after equipment of the period.

Donald was one of America's top competitive surfers during the 1960s. The talented goofy footers speed and classic Hawaiian style saw him consistently placed among the best surfers in the USA.

Takayamas company, Hawaiian Pro Designs, grew substantially during the longboard renaissance of the mid '80s. Longboarding was back in vogue and Donald's skill was in high demand. He made signature boards for some of the sports legends including Nat Young and David Nuuhiwa.

Featured in more than a dozen surf movies and the recipient of numerous awards, Donald has undoubtedly earned his place in the International Surfers' Hall of Fame. Presently Donald lives between Carlsbad, California and Molokai Hawaii, with his wife Diane. He continues to live the surfing lifestyle.

kevin kinnear

Surfers Choice Clam Chowder

A delicious meal perfect if you are feeding a large group of people. If you like your food spicy add a dash of tabasco. Makes approximately 12 one cup servings

ingredients

150g (5 oz) of diced bacon

1 large onion

6 medium potatoes

700ml (1.5 pints) of evaporated milk

2 ¼ cups of water

2 medium cans of creamed corn

700g (1.5 lb) of cleaned clams in shells

1 bunch of coriander/cilantro

Pepper and garlic salt to taste

method

• Dice onion. Wash, peel and chop potatoes into bite sized pieces.

• In a large pot sauté bacon and onion until cooked.

• Add evaporated milk, water, creamed corn and potatoes.

• Cover and cook on low to medium heat until potatoes are almost tender (approximately 45 minutes).

• Chop coriander and add to chowder along with salt, pepper and tabasco.

• Add clams and cook for a further 10 minutes (clams will open in shell when done).

• Serve with crusty sour dough or French bread. Yum!

Shinpei Horiguchi

Shinpei Horiguchi is undoubtedly one of the best Japanese surfers in history. The talented regular footer has earned a reputation for charging some of the world's most dangerous waves and towing into monstrous typhoon swells around his Japanese homeland.

Born in Hyogo Japan, Shinpei moved to his father's home town of Wakayama soon after. He began surfing at the age of seven. Lucky enough to grow up between the idyllic island locations of Japan and Hawaii, Horiguchi became comfortable riding large waves. Under the guidance of his father Genki, who still acts as his coach, Shinpei has made his dream of becoming a professional surfer a reality.

Although Horiguchi excels in all conditions he is most admired for his prowess at infamous big wave locations such as Sunset, Pipeline and Wiamea Bay. He has graced the cover of surfing magazines and is somewhat of a celebrity in Japan. Sponsored by several transnational surf wear companies, he spends his time traveling the world to chase waves and compete in surf contests. Presently living in Wakayama, Shinpei has kindly chosen to share his favorite soup recipe with us.

go-naminori.com

Chicken Vegetable Soup

Serves 4.

ingredients

200g (7 oz) of chicken	2 cloves of garlic
2 cups of white rice	6 cups of chicken stock
1 radish	3 shallots/spring onions
2 carrots	2 tablespoons of oil
1 large potato	2 tablespoons of sake
2 sticks of celery	Optional- soy sauce and dried binto shaving to taste
1 onion	

method

- Cook rice as desired. Set aside.
- Dice all vegetable and chicken.
- Heat a saucepan to medium and sauté onion and garlic in oil.
- Add chicken and cook for 2 minutes stirring constantly.
- Add all remaining vegetables and sake. Continue cooking for 3 minutes.
- Cover with chicken stock and season with salt and pepper.
- Add binto shavings and soy if desired.
- Place lid on saucepan and simmer until vegetables are tender.
- Serve in a bowl on top of steamed rice.

Dave Parmenter

Dave Parmenter is an accomplished author and respected surfboard shaper from California. During the 1980s Parmenter competed professionally on the ASP World Tour and since his 1990 retirement, has continuously pushed the boundaries of surfboard design.

Growing up on California's Central Coast, Parmenter taught himself to surf and by 1982 was one of America's top professionals. Competition however has never defined him. Dave has dedicated himself to enjoying the ocean on all forms of equipment and lists bodysurfing as his favourite form of wave riding. In the 1990s Dave moved to Hawaii where he created his surfboard brand, Aleutian Juice.

Parmenter has travelled extensively and in recent years has taken surfing to new frontiers. Dave, along with fellow waterman Brian Keaulana, has stand up paddle surfed in the Colorado River. His 1993 article *The Land Duke Forgot* focused media attention on Alaskan surfing for the first time.

Presently Parmenter is focused on his shaping and journalistic endeavors. He contributes to numerous surfing magazines and is presently one of the leaders of the stand up paddle movement.

allen mazo

Lazy Whitecap Ranch Guacamole

Dave's original guacamole recipe is easy to make and delicious served with corn chips and a cold beer.

ingredients
2 large ripe avocados (fruit must be firm and waxy, not
watery and stringy)
¼ cup of finely grated onion, preferably Maui onion
1 tablespoon of Worcestershire sauce
Juice of 1 lime
½ teaspoon of salt
1 bag of corn chips

method
• Spoon the avocado into a bowl and mash with a fork until smooth.
• Add remaining ingredients and continue stirring and mashing until a paste-like consistency is achieved.
• Smooth a sheet of plastic wrap over the dip and refrigerate for half an hour.
• Remove from fridge and stir again before serving.
• Serve with corn chips.

Rob Machado

tom servais

Rob Machado is the epitome of good style both in and out of the water. A musician, artist and infinitely talented surfer, Machado is known worldwide for his speed, fluidity, easy going attitude and massive fro.

Rob grew up in the seaside town of Cardiff, amongst some of Southern California's best waves. He entered his first surfing contest at age twelve and hasn't looked back since. During his professional career Rob won thirteen WQS and eight WCT contests, including the Pipeline Masters. Machado narrowly lost the 1995 World Title to Kelly Slater, where the pair traded perfect Pipeline tube rides and high fives. Although Slater was the eventual victor, their heat remains one of the most memorable in surfing history.

Machado has been featured in over fifty surf films including *Drifting: The Rob Machado Chronicles, Thicker than Water, Shelter* and *Momentum*. Since his retirement from full time competition Rob has become a professional free surfer, shifting his focus to photo and film trips.

A Surfing Hall of Fame inductee and philanthropist, Machado continues to give back to his community by hosting events and donating to numerous charities. Rob resides in his hometown of Cardiff with his family. He continues to surf daily and enjoys the ocean on a variety of equipment.

tom servais

Classic Nachos

The recipe below serves approximately 2-3, however quantities can easily be doubled for more people.

ingredients

1x 420g (15 oz) can of refried beans
2 tablespoons of cream cheese
1 large bag of corn chips
2 cups of grated cheese
150g (5 oz) tub of sour cream
Hot sauce to taste

Salsa
2 tomatoes
1 red onion
1 bunch of coriander/cilantro
½ a lemon
Guacamole see previous page

method

• Preheat oven to 180°C (350°F).
• In a bowl mix beans and cream cheese together. Heat in microwave for 90 seconds.
• Spread bean mixture evenly over base of a large oven-proof platter or baking dish.
• Stand corn chips vertically in beans and sprinkle with grated cheese.
• Bake in oven till cheese melts and chips are crisp.
• *Salsa:* Roughly chop tomatoes, onion and coriander. Mix together in a bowl with the juice of half a lemon. Season with salt and pepper.
• Spread salsa evenly over the top of chips and melted cheese.
• Garnish with dollops of sour cream and guacamole. Add hot sauce if desired.
• Serve immediately and enjoy with an extra bowl of corn chips on the side.

Gerry Lopez

tom servais

Gerry Lopez can be described as many things; world class tube rider, Indonesian surfing pioneer, snowboarder, executive, shaper and family man. Yet in the surfing world Lopez is most revered for his powerful elegance and absolute mastery of one of the worlds most dangerous waves, The Banzi Pipeline on Oahu's North Shore.

Although Lopez proved successful in the competitive arena, it was his free surfing that left people mesmerized. By the mid '70s Lopez's image dominated the surf media. Besides being featured in iconic surfing classics, such as *Morning of the Earth*, Lopez has inspired books, countless articles and appeared in Hollywood films such as *Big Wednesday* and *Conan the Barbarian*.

For the past eight years Gerry has been an ocean ambassador for environmentally minded sportswear giant Patagonia. He continues to surf, snowboard and has recently published a book titled, *Surf is Where You Find It*.

Lopez's achievements include being named shaper of the year, collaborating on tow-in equipment, co-founding Lightning Bolt Surfboards and being inducted into the Surfing Walk of Fame. Known as "Mr Pipeline", Gerry is undoubtedly one of the most influential surfers of his generation. His style both in and out of the water is inspirational.

tom servais

Brown Rice and Teriyaki Sauce

A delicious accompaniment to any meal, this simple recipe is a staple of a healthy diet. This teriyaki sauce works as an excellent marinade for tofu, fish, chicken or the meat of your choice. The 2:3 ratio for cooking rice works in rice cookers also.

ingredients

Brown Rice
2 cups of organic medium grain brown rice
3 cups of spring/filtered water

Teriyaki sauce
Tamari soy sauce
Honey
Crushed garlic
Finely ground ginger
Roasted sesame seeds

method
- *Brown Rice:* Wash rice thoroughly in strainer.
- Mix rice and water in a thick covered pot.
- Bring to rapid boil then turn your flame down to the lowest setting.
- Allow all the water to absorb, this should take 45-50 minutes.
- When the rice is done, take the lid off and stir with a wooden rice paddle and let the steam out. Serve.
- *Teriyaki sauce:* Mix ingredients to your own taste preference, some like more ginger and less garlic so experiment until you find what you like best. Stir into rice and enjoy!

Robert August

robertaugust.com

Robert August has been a surf star for over forty years. His performance in Bruce Brown's epic film, *The Endless Summer*, made Robert famous beyond the surf world. Since the movie, Robert has made a name and life for himself within the surfing industry as a successful shaper and shop owner.

Robert was born in 1945 to a father who was both a surfer and a lifeguard. He began surfing at six and by his early teens had acquired a reputation as one of California's most promising young surfers. After high school Robert was offered the opportunity to co-star in *The Endless Summer* with Mike Hynson. The film followed two young surfers travelling around the globe in search of perfect waves and perpetual summer. The film became an instant classic earning rave reviews and turning August into a pop icon.

Robert began shaping surfboards in 1966 and in 1974 opened his own shop. As longboards came back into fashion during the late '80s an increased demand for Robert August shapes developed.

Robert had a cameo appearance in the 1994 *Endless Summer II* and has been inducted into the Huntington Beach Surfing Walk of fame. Today Robert enjoys an idyllic lifestyle between his homes in California and Costa Rica.

robertaugust.com

Blanched Zucchini Squash

gutter photos

This recipe is quick, easy and feeds 6-8 adults as a side dish. You can alter the recipe to suit the number of people you are feeding.

ingredients
6 zucchinis
250g (9 oz) of pepper jack or cheddar cheese
½ cup of grated parmesan cheese
Pinch of salt

method
- Wash zucchinis and cut off ends.
- Bring a large pot of water to the boil. Add salt.
- Blanch zucchinis in water for 3 minutes then immediately rinse under cold tap.
- Cut zucchinis in half length ways.
- On the flat side of zucchini, cut a slit half way through flesh, from end to end.
- Insert a strip of pepper/cheddar cheese into length of the slit.
- Cover flat side with parmesan.
- Cook in oven or under griller until bubbling and golden brown.
- Season with salt and pepper. Serve.
- Eat with Robert August Pinot Grigio!

mains

Layne Beachley

sabine albers

Layne Beachley is statistically the greatest women's competitive surfer in history. She has overcome numerous obstacles to win an unprecedented seven world titles.

Beachley's many accolades include a Teen Choice Award, becoming Australian Female Athlete of the Year and being inducted into the Surfers' Hall of Fame. Layne has also proved to be a successful entrepreneur, creating Beachley Athletic, her own brand of functional active wear that aims to empower women.

Growing up on Sydney's Northern Beaches, Layne turned professional at the tender age of sixteen. She competed at surfing's highest level for over twenty years, winning the respect of her peers and the wider sporting community for her focus and training regime.

Admirably, Layne has used her profile to increase awareness of numerous charities and causes. She is an ambassador for The National Breast Cancer Foundation, SurfAid, Planet Ark and The Day Of Difference Foundation. Additionally, Layne has created her own Aim For the Stars Foundation, which helps young Australian women achieve their dreams.

After the 2008 season Layne officially retired from competition to focus on her business and charity work. Layne's commitment and focus have made her one of surfing's most successful and inspiring personalities.

sean collins

Tofu Fajitas

This yummy Mexican feast is both healthy and delicious. Serves 4.

ingredients

400g (14 oz) block of firm tofu

400g (14 oz) can of black or kidney beans

2 tablespoons of olive oil

1 red capsicum/bell pepper

2 zucchinis

1 onion

1 bunch of coriander/cilantro

1-2 avocados

1 fresh lime

1x 300g (10.5 oz) jar of tomato salsa

200g (7 oz) tub of sour cream

12 tortillas

Cumin powder, paprika powder
and chilli flakes to taste

method

- Preheat oven to 180°C (350°F).
- Dice tofu and sprinkle with cumin and paprika. Set aside.
- Roughly chop onion, capsicum and zucchini. Sauté with olive oil in a large frying pan or wok. Season to taste with cumin, paprika and chilli flakes.
- Add tofu and cook for another 5-10 minutes. Take off heat and cover.
- Wrap tortillas in foil or a cloth and heat for approximately 10 minutes until warm.
- In a separate bowl mash avocado with lime juice, two tablespoons of salsa and coriander. Season with salt and pepper.
- Place black beans in a bowl and heat until steaming.
- Wrap tofu mix, beans and guacamole in warm tortillas. Top with sour cream and salsa.
- Serve with Mexican rice if desired.

Ian Cairns

peter crawford

Ian "Kanga" Cairns has been involved in surfing as a competitor, coach, shaper, promoter and director. Famous for his prowess in huge waves and diplomatic handling of professional events, Cairns has dedicated his life to the development of surfing.

Although his introduction to the ocean began on Sydney's Northern Beaches, it was in Western Australia that Ian gained a reputation as one of Australia's best junior surfers. Charging the heavy waves WA is famous for, Cairns took a total of six state titles and competed in several World Surfing Championships.

In the early '70s Ian won numerous prestigious competitions including the 1973 Smirnoff Pro and 1975 Duke Classic. One of the world's best power surfers, Cairns excelled in the formidable Hawaiian waves winning both the 1976 and 1980 World Surfing Cups in pumping swells.

An intense supporter of professional surfing, Cairns was a co-founder of both the Australian Professional Surfing Association and Bronzed Aussies. As head coach of the NSSA, founder and first executive director of the ASP, Ian has been instrumental in surfing's expansion.

An inductee into the Australian Surfing Hall of Fame, the former stunt double and father of four calls California's Laguna Beach home. He remains committed to promoting surfing and gets in the water himself whenever he can.

mccormack

Garlic and Rosemary Lamb

ingredients

1.5kg (3.3 lbs) leg of lamb

6 cloves of garlic

1 sprig of fresh rosemary

6 potatoes

1 large piece of pumpkin/butternut squash

2 sweet potatoes/yams (1 if they are large)

Olive oil

Gravy

1 tablespoons of flour

1½ cups of beef or chicken stock

method

- Preheat oven to 200°C (400°F).
- Peel and cut potatoes, pumpkin and sweet potatoes into chunks. Slice garlic finely.
- Make 10 slits into lamb, place a little rosemary and a garlic slice into each.
- Lightly grease a large roasting pan with olive oil. Place lamb in pan, brush with oil and season with salt and pepper. Roast in oven for 15 minutes.
- Remove from oven and arrange the potatoes around the lamb in a single layer. Drizzle oil over potatoes, season with salt and pepper and bake for a further 30 minutes.
- Add the sweet potatoes and pumpkin. Again drizzle with oil and season.
- Sprinkle any remaining rosemary and garlic over roast. Cook for a further 40 minutes.
- Remove from oven. Transfer lamb to serving plate. Cover with foil and let it sit for ten minutes. Transfer vegetables to another greased baking dish and place back in the oven for 10 minutes.
- *Gravy:* Add flour to roast pan and cook over high heat stirring constantly until gravy bubbles.
- Gradually add stock and bring to boil. Keep stirring. Reduce heat slightly and cook for 5 minutes until gravy thickens.
- Slice lamb and serve with vegetables and gravy.

Adriano de Souza

swilly.com

Adriano de Souza is presently one of the finest surfers in the world. The talented Brazilian is highly regarded among his peers as one of the WCT's fiercest competitors.

Born in Sao Paulo, Brazil, the softly spoken de Souza began surfing at age eight. He developed his trademark lightning quick style amongst the beach breaks of Guarujá. After a stellar junior career, which included five state titles and the 2003 World Pro Junior Championship, Adriano graduated to the major leagues.

The demanding World Qualifying Series provided Adriano with the perfect opportunity to showcase his talent. The small wave aficionado dominated the tour winning the 2005 season convincingly. Despite doubts that de Souza may not translate his surfing to the elite WCT, he proved the critics wrong and adapted his style to the perfect waves of the ASP Dream Tour.

Adriano is one of the hardest working guys on tour. All the training has definitely paid off. In 2009 Adriano has achieved his highest ranking to date, reaching the position of world number two. As this talented South American is still only in his twenties, it's certain that the world will see a lot more of Mr de Souza.

swilly.com

Sesame Wasabi Tuna

This recipe is quick, easy and healthy. Best enjoyed with a crisp salad and teriyaki rice (see Gerry Lopez), recipe serves 4.

ingredients

4x 200g (7 oz) of fresh tuna steaks

⅔ cup of black and white sesame seeds

3 tablespoons of butter

3 teaspoons of wasabi paste

2 teaspoons of sesame oil

1 teaspoon of soy sauce

Soy sauce and pickled ginger to serve

Garnish with capsicum/bell peppers and shallots/scallions

method

- Heat butter in a frying pan until it starts to bubble.
- Add sesame seeds and cook till white seeds are golden brown.
- Remove pan from heat and add wasabi, sesame oil and soy sauce. Set aside.
- Heat another frying pan to high. Sear tuna for 1-2 minutes on each side to seal.
- Coat tuna in sesame seed mixture.
- Slice tuna into strips. Garnish with chopped capsicum and shallots.
- Serve with soy sauce and pickled ginger.

Rusty Keaulana

Rusty Keaulana is Hawaiian surfing royalty. A three time Longboard World Champion and respected big wave surfer, he is the epitome of a waterman.

Rusty grew up on Oahu's West Side. Keaulana's father, Buffalo, is a living legend and widely regarded as the Mayor of Makaha. One of Hawaii's first lifeguards, Buffalo was a successful competitive surfer in the '50s and '60s. Rusty's brother Brian has also followed in the family tradition becoming one of the most esteemed lifeguards in the world. In this environment it is no wonder Rusty became one of the most successful longboard surfers ever.

Keaulana did not just win three world titles, he helped usher in progressive longboard surfing. An accomplished competitor, Keaulana has proven himself on the global stage in a variety of conditions, winning his world titles in vastly different circumstances from pumping triple overhead Haleiwa to waist high Malibu.

Interestingly Keaulana is a switch-foot, meaning he can surf with either foot forward. This rare ability is one of the many things for which Rusty is admired. Keaulana has cemented his status as a first class big wave surfer and is a perennial invitee to the prestigious annual Eddie Aikau contest.

Loco Moco Burger

twaddlebean

The Loco Moco Burger is a Hawaiian favourite especially after a long surf. This recipe makes 1 burger so adjust it accordingly.

ingredients
1x 120g (4 oz) of ground beef or a hamburger patty
1 egg
1 cup of cooked rice
Gravy
1 large hamburger bun or bread roll

method
- Form the ground beef into a patty. In a frying pan over medium-high heat, cook patty to your liking. This may be from 3 to 10 minutes. Remove from heat and set aside.
- In the same pan cook the egg in the hamburger grease. It should be cooked sunny-side up or over easy, but again you can vary this to your liking.
- Cut the bun/bread roll in half and place a large scoop of rice on the bottom slice. Next layer on the hamburger patty and egg.
- Top with heated gravy. Season with salt and pepper.
- Place other half of bun on top and serve.

Rosy Hodge

Rosanne "Rosy" Hodge is one of the best female surfers on the planet. The five feet, ten inch tall regular footer is currently the only South African woman competing on the elite World Championship Tour.

Raised in the wave rich town of East London, South Africa, Rosy followed her father and brother into the ocean at age eight. An all round athlete, Hodge swam competitively earning her state colours. Rosy made the finals of the under tens boys division in the first national titles she ever entered. At just eleven she was selected to represent her country at the World Grommet Championships in Indonesia. Rosy got a taste of things to come as a teenage wildcard in several WCT events.

A nine time South African National Champion, Hodge managed to qualify for the WCT after just one year on the grueling World Qualifying Series; a remarkable feat. Undeniably one of the most marketable surfers on the women's tour, Rosy has the support of several multinational sponsors and is a positive role model for young African women.

When not travelling the world, Rosy enjoys being home with her family where she spends time reading, drawing or training for her next contest.

Chicken and Vegetable Pie

This is straight up comfort food. Serves approximately 8.

ingredients

1kg (2.2 lbs) of chicken thighs

2 tablespoons of butter or olive oil

2 large potatoes

2 carrots

2 zucchinis

1 cup of diced sweet potato/yams

1½ cups of frozen sweet baby peas

1 cup of diced pumpkin/butternut squash

1 cup of broccoli florettes

1 cup of cauliflower florettes

700g (1.5 lbs) ready made puff pastry

Cheese sauce

2 tablespoons of butter

3 tablespoons of plain flour

1½ cups of milk

1 cup of grated cheese

1 cup of ricotta cheese

Salt and pepper to taste

method

- Preheat oven to 200°C (400°F).
- Wash, peel and chop all vegetables into bite sized pieces.
- Boil or steam vegetables until tender. Drain and cool.
- Cut chicken thighs into bite sized pieces. Sauté chicken in butter or oil until just cooked.
- *Cheese sauce:* In saucepan melt butter on medium heat. Stir in flour and cook for 2 minutes stirring constantly. Slowly add milk. Stir continually till near boiling and thickened.
- Add grated cheese. Stir until melted, then add ricotta. Cool.
- Fold drained vegetables and chicken into cheese sauce. Season with salt and pepper.
- Grease a large pie dish with butter. Line with pastry.
- Spoon in filling and top with another layer of pastry. Press edges together with a fork.
- Poke several small breathing holes in top of pie before placing in oven.
- Bake for 45-50 minutes, until pastry is golden. Allow to sit for 10 minutes before serving.

Laurie Towner

Laurie Towner is the complete surfing package. Widely known for paddling into some of the world's most dangerous waves, Laurie excels in all conditions. Although he occasionally competes, Towner has the distinction of being a professional free surfer.

Raised in Angourie, Australia, Laurie perfected his style on the first class waves surrounding his home. Towner had considerable success as a junior, winning several competitions including events held at Raglan and the iconic Bells Beach. After his junior career, Laurie chose a different path to most gifted surfers and instead of slogging it out on the WQS chose to chase swells all over the globe.

Extremely comfortable in large surf, Laurie has always been a standout on Hawaii's North Shore. In winter 2006 he scored himself arguably the best wave of the season. The humble natural footer came to worldwide attention when he rode a monster wave at Tasmania's Shipsterns Bluff. His incredible feat landed him on the cover of Surfer Magazine and made Towner one of Australia's highest profile surfers outside of the WCT. In 2007 Laurie won the prestigious Surfer Poll Heavy Water award for his performance in Billabong's *Frothing*.

stuart gibson

Seafood Marinara

Please note that you can substitute your favourite type of fresh seafood into the recipe depending upon personal preference and availability. Serves 4.

ingredients

2 tablespoons of olive oil

3 garlic cloves

1 onion

250g (9 oz) of peeled and shelled prawns/shrimp

250g (9 oz) of scallops

200g (7 oz) of calamari

1x 600g (1.3 lbs) tin diced tomatoes

2 tablespoons of tomato paste

1 cup of white wine

1 teaspoon of dried oregano

500g (1.1 lb) packet of spaghetti or your favourite pasta

Garnish with finely chopped parsley

Salt and pepper to taste

method

• Heat oil to medium temperature in a large saucepan.
• Chop onion and garlic. Cook for 3 minutes.
• Add tomatoes, wine and oregano. Season with salt and pepper.
• Add seafood and simmer for 30 minutes until sauce thickens.
• While sauce is cooking prepare pasta according to packet directions.
• Serve marinara sauce on top of pasta. Garnish with parsley.

Randy Rarick

Randy Rarick is surfing's chameleon. During his almost fifty years in the surfing industry Randy has been a professional longboarder, contest organiser, surfboard shaper, shop owner, auctioneer and movie location scout. All while co-founding a professional surfing circuit and travelling to more countries than possibly any other surfer.

Rarick was raised in Hawaii and at the age of ten learned to surf under the tutelage of legendary Waikiki beach boy, Rabbit Kekai. Ever since, Randy's life has been based around his love for the ocean.

A successful competitor during the 60s and 70s, Randy is most famous for helping to establish the International Professional Surfers (IPS) world circuit with Fred Hemmings. The IPS eventually turned into the ASP, which presently organises all professional events. For over twenty five years Randy has run surfing's Hawaiian Triple Crown, the most prestigious series of contests in the world, held on Oahu's infamous North Shore.

Today Rarick lives a stones throw from Sunset Point with his wife, Jacque. He is an inspiration and continues to surf, shape, travel and contribute to the enrichment of surfing. Lucky for us, Jacque is an amazing cook who attended culinary school in France. This recipe is simply divine.

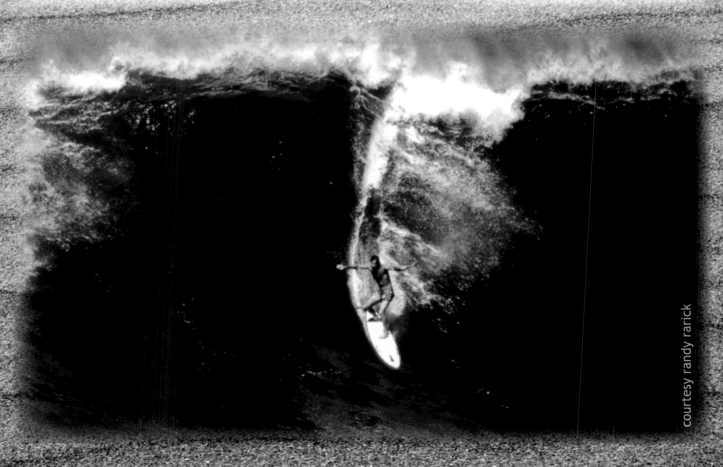

courtesy randy rarick

Mongolian Marinated Lamb Chops

Serves 4-6.

ingredients

⅓ cup of finely chopped shallots

⅓ cup of hoisin sauce

¼ cup of finely chopped fresh garlic

¼ cup of honey

¼ cup of creamy peanut butter

¼ cup of sesame oil

¼ cup of soy sauce

3 tablespoons of chopped fresh coriander/ cilantro

2 tablespoons of minced fresh ginger

Chilli sauce to taste

¼ cup of rice wine vinegar

¾ cup of sherry wine vinegar

1-2 racks of lamb

method

• Mix all ingredients together except the vinegars. (As they will actually start to "cook" the lamb if you put them in too early).

• Cut racks of lamb into chops, removing any excess fat.

• Marinate chops in fridge for at least 6 hours before cooking.

• Add the vinegars approximately 1 hour before you're ready to start cooking meat.

• Heat your BBQ to medium.

• Cook them for about 5 minutes on each side, depending on how "well done" you like your meat. Enjoy!

Joel Parkinson

Joel Parkinson is absolutely mesmerising in the ocean. Famous for making the most difficult manoeuvres look effortless; Parkinson is one of the most stylish surfers of the modern era.

Joel was introduced to surfing at the age of three. After an adolescent move to the surfing Mecca of Queensland's Gold Coast, Parkinson became one of the "Cooly Kids" along with fellow child prodigies Mick Fanning and Dean Morrison. The best mates dominated the amateur surfing scene, with Joel winning two World Junior Championships in 1999 and 2001.

Parkinson's surfing repertoire combines aerial ability and power with a smooth stylishness reminiscent of Tom Curren. Joel made a stunning professional debut, winning the prestigious Jeffries Bay Pro as an eighteen year old wildcard. Since his first year on the WCT in 2001, Joel has had numerous victories and been ranked as high as number one. Known as the surfer's surfer, Parkinson has starred in dozens of films including headlining *Free as a Dog* in 2006.

Despite his success Parkinson remains true to his roots enjoying BBQ's, football and spending time with friends. Presently residing in Coolangatta with his wife, Monica and their two young daughters, Parkinson is currently at the top of his game and seems destined for a world title.

The Ultimate Fish Marinade

This delicious marinade is perfect for any type of fish. Recipe serves 4.

ingredients

½ cup of soy sauce

2 limes

3 tablespoons of olive oil

3 cloves of garlic

3 tablespoons of grated ginger

2 tablespoons of light brown sugar

4 fish fillets

method

• Chop garlic finely, juice limes and grate ginger.
• Combine soy sauce, lime juice, oil, garlic, ginger and sugar together in a bowl. Mix well.
• Place fish in marinade and refrigerate for at least 2 hours prior to cooking.
• Cook fish as desired (BBQ, fry, grill, or roast).
• Serve with a salad and good quality white wine.

Linda Benson

john elwell

Linda Benson is a surfing icon. The petite blonde was one of the first women to take on the massive waves of Waimea Bay and experienced colossal competitive success throughout the 1960s.

Benson grew up in Encinitas, California and began surfing at age eleven. Less than five years later Linda became the youngest person to ever enter the International Championships at Makaha; which she won convincingly.

Although renowned for her small wave style, Benson earned the respect of the surfing community when she ventured into the enormous waves of Oahu's North Shore as a teenager. Throughout the '60s Linda competed extensively in both the tandem and individual divisions. A five time American Champion and runner up to the 1964 World Title, Linda was the first woman to ever appear on the cover of a surfing magazine.

Bud Brown and John Severson featured Linda in numerous iconic surf films of the '60s. She was also a stunt double in several Hollywood movies such as *Gidget Goes Hawaiian*.

A flight attendant for thirty five years, Linda remains active in the surfing community as an ambassador for Women's Longboarding. An inductee into both The Surfing Walk and Hall of Fame, Linda continues to get in the ocean whenever she can.

tom keck

California Kebabs with Couscous

twaddlebean

Serves 3-4.

ingredients

Kebabs

3 chicken breasts sliced thinly or 600g
(1.3 lb) of chicken tenders

16 button mushrooms

2 zucchinis

2 onions

3 tablespoons of olive oil

2 teaspoons of balsamic vinegar

8 bamboo skewers

Couscous

1x 165g (6 oz) package of couscous

1 tablespoon of olive oil

½ cup of chopped spring onions

1½ teaspoons of minced ginger root

1 small carrot

1 cup of broccoli florets

1 teaspoon of sesame oil

2 tablespoons of light soy sauce

method

• *Kebabs*: Soak skewers in water while you prepare vegetables.
• Cut chicken and vegetables into large bite size pieces. Season with garlic salt and pepper.
• Thread onto skewers alternating between chicken and vegetables.
• Mix olive oil and vinegar in a bowl and brush over the kebabs. Cook kebabs on grill for approximately 12 minutes turning occasionally until cooked through.
• *Couscous*: Prepare couscous according to package directions. Fluff lightly with fork.
• Chop all vegetables into small pieces.
• Heat frying pan to medium and add oil. Add onions, ginger, carrots and broccoli. Cook for 3-4 minutes or until tender. Stir into couscous. Add sesame oil and soy. Toss.
• Serve kebabs on a bed of couscous.

Phil Rajzman

Phil Rajzman was the first Brazilian ASP World Surfing Champion. His 2007 win at the Longboarding World Championships in Anglet, France, made him a hero in his homeland, bringing long awaited surfing glory to Brazil. Phil's friendly nature and skill in the water make him one of longboarding's most popular personalities.

Phil spent his formative years in his hometown of Rio de Janeiro, in addition to travelling extensively. Phil's father, a professional volleyball player, competed all over the world often taking Phil along. Obviously athletic skill was in some part hereditary because by the age of fifteen Phil was winning surfing contests and being touted as one of Brazil's most promising juniors.

Phil does not limit himself to riding one style of surfboard and has had competitive success on both long and shortboards. Talented in the water regardless of the conditions, he is always exciting to watch. Besides his obvious surfing accomplishments, Phil is also a martial arts expert in jujitsu and trains ultimate fighters.

Phil learned this delectable pasta recipe while living in Italy. It's great enjoyed with a glass of wine and some hot crunchy bread.

Mushroom and Artichoke Fettuccine

twaddlebean

Serves 4-6.

ingredients

4 vegetable stock cubes

3 tablespoons of olive oil

2 large onions

6 cloves of garlic

1x 200g (7 oz) jar of artichoke hearts

200g (7 oz) of mushrooms

½ cup of white wine

½ cup of water

1 cup of fresh cream at room temprature

500g (1.1 lb) packet of fettuccini or your favourite type of pasta

Parmesan cheese to serve

method

• Chop garlic and onion finely.

• Chop artichoke hearts and mushrooms roughly.

• Heat olive oil in saucepan. Sauté garlic till golden brown. Add onions and water. Stir.

• Add artichoke hearts, mushrooms, wine and two stock cubes.

• Simmer for 5-10 minutes.

• Add two stock cubes to a large pot full of water. Bring water to the boil and add pasta.

• Cook per instructions on packet. Drain and set aside.

• Let sauce cool slightly then add cream.

• Serve pasta on large plate. Top with sauce and fresh grated parmesan cheese.

Joey Cabell

Joey Cabell was one of the most successful surfers of the 1960s. He managed a triumphant surfing career while simultaneously ski racing, earning a degree and co-founding the extremely successful Chart House restaurant chain.

Cabell grew up in Hawaii where he began surfing at age seven. As a kid hanging out at Waikiki, Cabell was influenced by some of the greatest watermen of all time, such as Duke Kahanamoku, Rabbit Kekai and George Downing. It was in this environment that Cabell honed his extraordinary talent and unique speed focused style.

The exceptional thing about Joey was his ability to excel in a diverse range of waves and conditions. He won contests easily, regardless of wave size. Joey's polished grace and speed earned him his nickname, "The Gazelle".

Today Cabell, a father of three, spends his winters carveboarding in Colorado and summers surfing and sailing in Hawaii. At seventy years young Joey is still ripping it up in the waves and on the snow. His recipe is the delicious Kimmi's Firecracker Unroll, one of the specialties of The Honolulu Chart House.

bill romerhaus

74

Kimmi's Firecracker Unroll

Recipe serves 2.

ingredients

2 cups of cooked white rice

300g (10.5 oz) of fresh yellow fin tuna (ahi)

1 teaspoon of sea salt

½ cup of ogo Hawaiian seaweed

2 teaspoons of sesame oil

A pinch of dried chilli flakes

2 tablespoons of diced spring onions

2 tablespoons of soy sauce

½ cup of sweet round onion chopped julienne (long thin strips)

¾ cup of mayonnaise

2 teaspoons of chilli garlic sauce (with seeds)

Roasted Korean nori

Kizami (red ginger)

Kaiware (radish) sprouts without roots

method

• In a container combine mayonnaise and chilli garlic sauce. Taste, if you like it more spicy, add extra chilli garlic sauce, less spicy, add mayonnaise. Set aside.

• Cube tuna and place in a large bowl.

• Add sea salt, ogo, sesame oil, chilli, green and white onions and soy sauce to tuna. Toss.

• Place medium size scoop of white rice on each plate.

• Top the rice with the tuna mixture and drizzle with chilli mayonnaise.

• Cut nori into strips and arrange on top.

• Garnish with kaiware sprouts and kizami.

Julian Wilson

Julian Wilson is one of Australia's most innovative surfers. He has made a considerable impact on the surfing world by inventing a new maneuver, scoring perfect tens and winning the 2006 ISA World Junior Title.

Growing up amongst a surfing family in Coolum Queensland, it seemed inevitable that Julian would surf. Yet his talent is unprecedented. Amazing on both long and shortboards, his numerous contest wins and exciting free surfing have made Julian one of the worlds most talked about surfers. He has competed amongst the best including legends such as Kelly Slater.

Julian's resume also includes the invention of a new aerial manoeuvre called the "Sushi Roll" and surfing in front of 125, 000 people in a Malaysian wave pool. His segment in Quiksilver's *Young Guns 3* film, earned him the prestigious Best Male Performance at the Surfer Poll Awards.

Currently Julian is working on his much anticipated signature film before launching an assault on the competitive surfing world full time. Wilson is so immensely talented there is no limit to what he can achieve.

Julian has chosen to include his Mum Nola's famous Tango Mango Chicken. She says this is quick, tasty and easy after a fun day in the sea, doing whatever makes you happy.

Tango Mango Chicken

gutter photos

Serves 4.

ingredients

1kg (2.2 lbs) of chicken thighs

1 cup of plain flour

1x 500g (1.1 lb) tin of mangoes

1 fresh mango

1 orange squeezed

2 tablespoons of margarine/butter

method

- Coat chicken in flour.
- Cut fresh mango into bite sized pieces.
- In a heavy based frying pan melt margarine.
- Sauté chicken till cooked through. Remove from pan.
- Add tinned and fresh mangoes to pan juices. Squeeze in orange juice.
- Gently simmer until sauce thickens to preferred consistency
- Add chicken and stir.
- Serve over rice or pasta

Bob McTavish

mctavish.com.au

Bob McTavish is one of the most influential surfboard shapers of all time. A key player in the shortboard revolution and professional competitor in the 1960s, Bob remains one of surfing's most innovative characters.

Growing up in the sunshine state of Queensland, Australia, Bob began surfing at age twelve on a plywood paddleboard. It was true love. He left school to pursue the surfing dream and started shaping at seventeen.

McTavish was one of Australia's top competitive surfers throughout the early '60s, winning three Queensland state titles and being consistently placed highly in national competitions. Bob's many adventures include stowing away on a ship bound for Hawaii and being amongst the first to realize Noosa's epic potential.

At the forefront of progressive surfboard design for over forty years, Bob has played a key role in surfing's development. An inductee into the Australian Surfing Hall of Fame, the father of five resides in Byron Bay, NSW, where he surfs and shapes daily.

Bob's love affair with chilli rellenos started in Ventura, California back in 1968. After sampling many chilli rellenos in restaurants throughout America, Bob discovered the ultimate taste sensation in Castroville CA. Much experimentation in his Aussie kitchen led to his perfection of the recipe that he has kindly shared with us.

mctavish.com.au

Chilli Rellenos

Recipe serves 4.

ingredients

8 large green pasilla or banana chillies

200g (7 oz) of cheddar or jack cheese

1 cup of plain flour

½ teaspoon of bi-carb or baking soda

½ teaspoon of baking powder

½ cup of buttermilk

1 egg

¼ teaspoon of salt

Oil for frying

8 tortillas (flour or corn)

Tomato salsa either store bought or homemade (see Rob Machado)

1x 400g (14 oz) can of black, refried or kidney beans

method

• Heat oven to 200°C (400°F). Roast chillies for 5 minutes. Remove from oven.
• Rough up chilli skin with a fork to enable batter to adhere.
• Remove any skin that comes away easily.
• Make a small slit in chilli and carefully extract seeds.
• Inset a strip of cheese into each chilli. Gently press together.
• To prepare batter, place soda, baking powder, buttermilk, egg and salt in a large bowl.
• Mix together until combined.
• Coat each chilli in flour then dip in batter.
• Fry in oil until golden brown.
• Serve with warmed tortillas, beans, salsa and rice.

Sofia Mulanovich

Sofia Mulanovich is a remarkable surfer. She made history in 2004 when she became the first ever ASP World Surfing Champion, not only from her native Peru, but from the continent of South America.

Sofia's outstanding talent was discovered at a young age and nurtured by her surfing family and Peruvian champion, Magoo de la Rosa. In this supportive environment Mulanovich's surfing flourished.

Winning the 1998 Pan American Championships was a milestone for Sofia. She turned pro the next year and qualified for the elite WCT in 2002. Sofia's dream of becoming the best surfer in the world came true when she won her World Title in 2004. She dedicated her win to Peru, becoming a national hero and giving hope to little girls everywhere.

Besides her World Title, Sofia has achieved numerous accolades including six illustrious Surfer Poll Awards and a 2007 induction into the Surfers Hall of Fame. Her success inspired the critically acclaimed film *Sofia- A Documentary*, which chronicled a year in her life.

Mulanovich's humble personality and desire to give back have made her a South American ambassador. She is without a doubt, a beautiful and inspiring spokesperson for surfing.

Peruvian Ceviche

Ceviche is a delicious dish native to Latin America. This recipe serves 4-6 and is best made with freshly caught fish. It is impossible to burn as it requires no cooking!

ingredients

900g (2 lb) of your favourite fresh white fish fillets

6 garlic cloves

¼ cup of fresh chopped coriander/cilantro

1 habanero chilli (other types of chilli can be substituted)

1x 300g (10.5 oz) tin of corn kernels

10-12 limes juiced (there must be enough to cover fish)

1 red onion

1 teaspoon of salt

¼ teaspoon of pepper

1 packet of crackers

method

• Rinse the fish in fresh water and dry. Cut fish into bite sized cubes
• Thinly slice garlic and chilli (remove seeds).
• Combine all ingredients in a large bowl except onion. Ensure lime juice covers fish.
• Slice onion thinly and arrange over dish.
• Cover bowl and place in refrigerator to marinate for one and a half to two hours.
• Serve with crackers.

Matthew Moir

brenton geach

Matthew Moir is one of the most likeable characters in surfing. A veteran of the World Longboard Tour, Moir has been International Surfing Association (ISA) World Champion twice and has six South African National Titles to his credit.

Nicknamed "Mouse", Moir grew up amongst the epic waves of Cape Town, South Africa. With the support of his family, Matthew quickly established himself as a versatile competitor and one of the continent's best surfers.

The talented goofy footer has won numerous titles and contests. Besides his ISA and National Championship triumphs, Mouse has won the prestigious Rabbit Keikai Costa Rican Pro and came third in the ASP World Longboard Championship in 2003, 2004 and 2005. Despite his success Mouse remains humble, saying that the best part of competing is travelling to exotic destinations and meeting new people.

Matthew has gained friends and fans due to his outgoing nature and friendliness. He presently remains in Cape Town where he lives with his family. Matthew's wife, Kim, has shared her Bacon Wrapped Chicken Breast recipe, which is one of his favourite meals.

brenton geach

Bacon Wrapped Chicken Breast

gutter photos

Recipe serves 4.

ingredients

3 tablespoons of olive oil

2 cloves of garlic

4 chicken breasts

4 slices of mozzarella cheese

4 rashers of bacon

4 toothpicks

2 tablespoons of butter

1 cup of grated cheese

2 cups of milk

2 tablespoons of flour

Salt and pepper to taste

method

- Preheat oven to 180°C (350°F).
- Crush garlic and heat with oil in a medium sized pan.
- Brown the chicken breasts slightly then set aside to cool.
- Cut the chicken breast through lengthways but be sure to leave it attached on one side.
- Place a mozzarella slice inside each chicken breast.
- Wrap bacon around each chicken breast and secure with a toothpick.
- Place on baking tray and cook for approximately 15-20 minutes until bacon is crisp and chicken cooked through.
- *Cheese Sauce:* Melt butter in saucepan over medium heat. Add flour and stir to form a smooth paste. Cook for approximately 2 minutes stirring constantly.
- Gradually add milk. Keep stirring. Cook until thickened.
- Add salt, pepper and cheese. Stir until cheese melts.
- Pour over chicken and serve with your favourite side dish.

Bede Durbidge

andrew shield

Over the last five years Bede Durbidge has earned worldwide recognition for his incredible surfing. In 2008 Bede finished the year runner up to Kelly Slater, however he undoubtedly has the potential to win surfing's highest honour.

Raised in a close knit family on Queensland's Stradbroke Island, Bede had a variety of first class waves on which to hone his skills. After considerable success as a junior Bede competed on the exhaustive WQS. In 2005 Durbidge exploded onto the World Circuit Tour, he has since won a slew of competitions and beaten some of the sports biggest legends. Besides having being ranked an impressive world number two, Bede won the prestigious Pipeline Masters and Hawaiian Triple Crown in 2007.

The friendly Aussie is undoubtedly the complete surfing package. From airs to powerful hacks and graceful barrels, Durbidge does it all with finesse and fluidity. Admired by many for his cool in the heat of competition, Bede trains hard to enhance his natural ability. As Durbidge is arguably coming into the peak of his career it will be extremely interesting to see just how much this surfing powerhouse can achieve. Presently residing on the Gold Coast with his wife, Bede has kindly shared his taco recipe.

swilly.com

Beef Tacos

Serves 4.

ingredients

10 taco shells (hard or soft)

1 tablespoon of oil

500g (1.1 lb) of beef mince

2 cups of grated cheese

1 lettuce

Salsa

1 can of peeled whole tomatoes

2 cloves of garlic

Cumin powder

½ cup of chopped coriander/cilantro

Guacamole

2 ripe (almost soft) avocados

1 teaspoon of lime juice

½ cup of chopped coriander/cilantro

1 tomato

Sour cream optional

method

• Heat oven to 180°C (350°F).
• Shred lettuce. Set aside.
• Heat oil in a large frying pan on high temperature. Add meat and cook till brown and tender. Season with salt and pepper.
• *Salsa:* Drain tomatoes and combine with remaining ingredients in food processor or blender. Pulse quickly just 2-3 times or until desired consistency is reached. Add extra cumin and salt to taste. Place in bowl and set aside.
• Bake tacos in oven, according to package directions, until warm and crispy.
• *Guacamole:* Peel avocado and chop into small pieces. Mash into an almost smooth consistency. Finely dice tomato and stir into avocado with coriander. Mix in lime juice to avoid browning. Set aside.
• Serve tacos with mince, cheese, lettuce, salsa and guac. Add sour cream if you wish.

Wayne "Rabbit" Bartholomew

Wayne "Rabbit" Bartholomew is a World Champion and professional surfing pioneer who went onto become ASP President. It is due to his initiative, entertaining antics and larger than life personality that competitive surfing, as we know it, came into existence.

Rabbit was lucky enough to grow up on Australia's Gold Coast, famous throughout the surfing world for its perfect right-hand point breaks. The Goldy provided the ideal environment for the young natural footer to hone his skill along with greats, Peter Townend and Michael Peterson.

Although undoubtedly talented in the water, the unique thing about Bartholomew was his holistic attitude towards competitive surfing. As a result Rabbit became one of the most successful competitors of the '70s and won the 1978 World Title.

Since his retirement from competition in 1988, Rabbit has been a surf coach, environmental lobbyist and President of the ASP. His successful autobiography *Bustin' Down the Door* received critical acclaim.

Rabbit hasn't lost all his old competitive instincts, taking out several ASP Masters and Grand Masters Championships in recent years. All in all Rabbit has been a vital contributor to the sport and remains one of surfing's most iconic characters.

dick hoole

Salmon Toro Bowl

gutter photos

This recipe serves 2.

ingredients

2 cups of cooked rice

400g (14 oz) of fresh raw salmon

½ cup of seaweed

2 shallots/scallions

Wasabi to taste

Soy sauce

Fresh or pickled ginger

method

• Place rice in the bottom of a medium sized bowl.
• Cut salmon into bite sized pieces.
• Finely chop seaweed and onions.
• Arrange salmon pieces on top of rice.
• Sprinkle salmon with seaweed and onion.
• In a small dish mix wasabi and soy to taste.
• Serve with fresh or pickled ginger on the side and a hot cup of miso soup or green tea.

Simon Anderson

Simon Anderson forever changed surfing. A successful competitor and innovative shaper, Simon invented the thruster fin set-up. By putting three equal sized fins on a surfboard Simon not only transformed board design, but altered the way waves have been ridden ever since.

Anderson grew up amongst an athletic family in Sydney's Northern Beaches. After receiving a surfboard for his thirteenth birthday Simon's natural talent in the water became obvious. He was Australian Junior Champion several times, all while learning to shape surfboards. Anderson graduated to the professional level and at six feet, three inches tall, gained a reputation as one of Australia's best power surfers.

Simon came up with the thruster concept in 1980. At the time, twin fins were extremely popular however they were not stable enough to suit Simon's powerful surfing. The additional fin combined the twin fin's manoeuvrability with the single fin's drive. The idea proved a success. Simon won several of the world's most prestigious competitions on the thruster including The Bells Beach Classic and Pipeline Masters.

Since his retirement from professional surfing, Anderson has continued to make beautifully crafted, state of the art surfboards. Today Simon lives in Sydney with his family where he runs his own business and surfs whenever the waves permit.

basesurfboards.com

Chicken Laksa

Recipe serves 6 adults.

ingredients

1 clove of garlic

Small knob of ginger

2 cups of vegetables cut into small pieces, (recommended- broccoli, carrot, zucchini, cauliflower and corn)

3 tablespoons of olive oil

4 shallots/scallions

½ a red capsicum/bell pepper

3 tablespoons of laksa paste

1x 400ml (14 oz) can of coconut milk

400g (14 oz) of chicken (thighs or breasts)

8-10 button mushrooms

2 whole coriander/cilantro plants

800 ml (1.7 pints) of chicken or vegetable stock

200g (7 oz) of precooked noodles (rice or udon)

200g (7 oz) of bean sprouts

method

• Chop capsicum and mushrooms into bite sized pieces.
• Chop garlic, ginger and shallots finely. Cook in olive oil over medium heat in a wok or saucepan. Add laksa paste. Stir.
• Cut chicken into bite sized pieces and add to pan.
• Brown chicken then remove from heat. Pick out chicken pieces then set aside.
• Turn heat down to low. Place pan back on heat, add coconut milk and stir.
• Clean whole coriander plant and separate leaves. Chop root and stem finely.
• Add mushrooms, coriander stems and roots. Simmer for 2-4 minutes.
• Add stock and the rest of the vegetables. Simmer for 5 minutes.
• Add the chicken for additional 2 minutes.
• Add noodles, coriander leaves, bean sprouts and 1 more shallot finely sliced.
• Continue simmering for 2 minutes. Ensure chicken is cooked through.
• Serve in a large bowl. Garnish with a slice of lemon.

Ben Dunn

bendunn.com.au

Ben Dunn is one of Australia's rising stars. His immense talent has seen him quickly climb the ranks of competitive surfing, becoming one of the youngest males ever to qualify for the elite WCT Dream Tour.

Raised on Australia's East Coast amongst the consistently good waves of Old Bar, he began surfing at the age of six. Ben's Dad, Martin, is one of Australia's most respected surf coaches and played an instrumental part in his son's surfing development. Ben's natural ability, combined with hard work and focus, saw him dominate amateur competition. Dunn's junior career is undoubtedly one of the most successful in Australian history, culminating in two World Junior Titles.

The natural footer proved he was among the worlds best when he qualified for the ASP World Championship Tour in 2006. Since then Ben has overcome injury to be consistently placed in the world's top twenty.

Dunn's drive, competitive savvy and outstanding ability in the ocean make him one of Australia's most promising surf stars. His style has attracted the attention of fans and sponsors alike. Ben has contributed one of his favourite meals.

carl muxlow

Sausage Crock Pot Stew

gutter photos

This sausage crock-pot meal is a great variation of the classic 'Bangers and Mash' and will satisfy the most starving of surfers.

ingredients

Stew

6-8 thick sausages

2 tablespoons of olive oil

1 onion

2 carrots

1 sweet potato/yam

1 cup of frozen peas

1 cup of water

1 tablespoon of honey

1 packet of master foods sausage hot pot mix

(or season with your favourite herbs and spices)

Mashed Potatoes

4 large (about 1kg) potatoes

2 tablespoons of butter

½ cup of cream

Salt and pepper to taste

method

• *Sausage stew:* Cut sausages and vegetables into bite sized pieces
• In a frying pan cook sausage in olive oil until slightly brown. Add onion and cook together for approximately 5 minutes.
• Transfer sausage mix into crock pot (slow cooker).
• Add vegetables, hot pot sachet (herbs/spices), water and honey. Cook on high setting for approximately 4 hours or on low setting for 8 hours. Stir occasionally if your home.
• *Mashed potatoes:* Peel and roughly chop potatoes.
• Boil or steam potatoes until tender.
• Mash until smooth then add cream, butter, salt and pepper.
• Serve sausage stew on a bed of mashed potatoes.

Kim Hamrock

dangerwomen.com

Kim Hamrock is a mother, artist, businesswoman and World Champion surfer. Known as "Danger Woman" for her gutsy performances in the water, Kim is one of America's most successful competitors.

Hamrock began surfing at the age of sixteen. A Californian local, she didn't enter her first contest until 1990 at the age of thirty. However, success came quickly for this late bloomer. Entering longboard and shortboard competitions, the athletic goofy footer won the US shortboard title in 1993 and 1994. In 1995 and 1996 Hamrock pulled off the ultimate double, winning both the short and longboard divisions. In addition to winning an amazing twelve USA National Titles and the 2002 World Longboard Championship, Hamrock has won the 2005 Women's Pipeline Championships and been runner-up in the 2005 XXL Big Wave Awards.

Besides her competitive accomplishments, Hamrock is a master surf instructor. A director of the NSSIA, she also writes and produces instructional surf films. In 2005 Kim received her much deserved induction into the Surfing Walk of Fame.

A gifted artist, Kim is now focused on expressing her creative side. Presently Hamrock is probably in some tropical location where she continues to ride waves, paint, write, play guitar and enjoy life to the fullest.

ruben piña

Basil Shrimp Pasta

Serves 4.

ingredients

450g (1 lb) of your favourite pasta

450g (1 lb) cooked prawns/jumbo shrimp

¼ cup of olive oil

½ cup of basil leaves

2 cloves of garlic

2 tablespoons of sesame seeds

1 small eggplant

¼ cup of butter

2 serrano chillies

1 red onion

⅔ cup room temperature cream (optional)

Cayenne Pepper

Parmesan cheese

method

• Finely chop basil, garlic, chillies, eggplant and onion.

• Heat saucepan to high and add olive oil.

• Fry basil, garlic and sesame seeds.

• Add butter, chillies, onion and shrimp/prawns. Sauté until all ingredients are cooked.

• While sauce is cooking prepare pasta according to package directions. Set aside.

• If desired add cream to sauce during the last minute or so of cooking.

• Pour the sauce over the pasta and toss.

• Sprinkle with cayenne pepper and parmesan cheese. Garnish with basil.

• Serve with a garden salad and a glass of your favourite wine.

Damien Hobgood

tom servais

Damien Hobgood is an extremely talented goofy footer who has been consistently placed highly in surfing's World Championship Tour. Although a fantastic surfer regardless of the conditions, Damien excels in heavy left reef breaks and seems most at home in some of the worlds most infamous waves such as Cloudbreak, Pipeline and Teahupoo.

Damien was raised in Satellite Beach, Florida where he began surfing at the age of six with his twin brother CJ. Both brothers were standouts in junior competitions and eventually turned pro. Today the Hobgoods go down in history as the first siblings to ever simultaneously achieve top ten results. The brothers presently co-own a successful surf shop in Florida.

Throughout his career Damien has proved professionally resilient. He has overcome repetitive shoulder dislocations and surgery to compete on surfing's biggest stage. Hobgood was named rookie of the year in 2000 and has received numerous accolades for his impressive aerial surfing.

Damien presently lives with his wife Charlotte, and their beautiful children, in California. Charlotte has been kind enough to share their family favourite Portobello Mushroom Burger recipe. It is absolutely delectable.

swilly.com

Portobello Mushroom Burgers

twaddlebean

This recipe can easily be turned into a vegetarian main course simply by omitting the prosciutto. Serves 4.

ingredients

4 portobello mushrooms

1 tablespoon of olive oil

1 teaspoon of balsamic vinegar

Salt and pepper

125g (4.5 oz) of rocket/arugula

200g (7 oz) jar of roasted capsicum/bell peppers

½ cup of pine nuts

1½ cups of grated parmesan cheese

200g (7 oz) can of artichoke hearts

4 large slices of mozzarella cheese

8 pieces of prosciutto

method

• Preheat oven to 200°C (400°F).

• Wash mushrooms, take stems off and place on a baking sheet.

• Drizzle with olive oil and balsamic vinegar. Season with salt and pepper.

• Place in oven for 15 minutes, or until roasted.

• Cut artichoke hearts and capsicum into bite sized pieces. Slice mozzerella.

• In a large bowl, mix rocket, capsicum, pine nuts, parmesan cheese, artichoke hearts and salt and pepper to taste.

• When mushrooms are cooked, place 2 pieces of prosciutto on top of each mushroom.

• Layer salad mixture over prosciutto and top with mozzarella cheese.

• Put back in oven and cook until cheese melts.

• Serve hot with your favored side.

Taylor Jensen

Taylor Jensen is one of the most exciting longboard surfers of the modern era. His huge airs and fierce competitive performances have seen him claim the US Open of Surfing twice, along with the 2009 Australian Longboard Qualifying Series and two ASP North American Titles.

Jensen grew up in San Diego's Coronado, where he began surfing at the age of six. He entered his first contest at twelve and has been competing ever since. At six feet, five inches and 200 pounds, Jensen's athletic build helped him excel in numerous sports, but it was surfing that captured his heart.

Jensen turned pro at seventeen and had success almost immediately. What sets him apart from his contemporaries is his ability to launch massive airs on a longboard, land, then continue riding the wave. Jensen is regarded as the first longboarder to consistently accomplish the extremely difficult "Superman Air". Besides his aerial prowess Taylor also possesses the complete repertoire of traditional nose rides and powerful turns, making him one of the world's best longboard surfers.

Taylor's parents, Karen and Marty, own the historic Coronado Boathouse restaurant. They have allowed us to print a variation of their famous Macadamia Nut Crusted Halibut which is one of Taylor's favourites.

Macadamia Nut Crusted Halibut

coronado-boathouse.com

Serves 4.

ingredients

4 halibut steaks

1x 400ml (14 oz) can of coconut milk

1½ cups of semi crushed macadamia nuts

½ cup of breadcrumbs (Japanese panko breadcrumbs preferably)

2 tablespoons of rice flour

½ cup of clarified butter/ghee

4 slices of mango pureed (can be fresh, canned or frozen)

Peanut sauce to serve

Teriyaki sauce to serve

method

• Preheat oven to 180°C (350°F).

• Combine macadamia nuts, breadcrumbs, rice flour and clarified butter in a bowl.

• Mix together and set aside.

• Bake halibut in coconut milk for 7-8 minutes.

• Pull out of oven and top with macadamia mix.

• Put it back in the oven for another 2-3 minutes until crust is golden brown.

• Drizzle a large plate with peanut sauce. Add fish and top with teriyaki and mango puree.

• Serve with crusty bread and your preferred side.

Laird Hamilton

tim mckenna

Laird Hamilton is the ultimate waterman. His mind-boggling talent in the ocean on any type of equipment has made Laird an icon beyond the surfing world. He has invented sports, refined tow in surfing and ridden the millennium wave. The possibilities of what this man can accomplish seem limitless.

Laird was lucky enough to grow up with two surfing parents. His mother, Joanne, moved the family to Hawaii when Laird was a baby. His father, '60s surfing pioneer Bill Hamilton, inspired Laird to be an all round waterman. Laird now seems to be the personification of this concept.

At six feet, three inches and 215 pounds Laird enjoys the ocean on numerous types of equipment. He shortboards, bodysurfs, longboards, kite surfs, paddleboards and windsurfs. Additionally Hamilton chases 100 foot plus swells all over the globe.

Laird has appeared in innumerable magazines, been named The 2004 Waterman of the Year and one of People magazines Fifty Most Beautiful People. He is a technical advisor for Oxbow sportswear and a co-founder of BamMan Films. Laird has even created his own clothing line.

When Hamilton is not riding monster waves, wind surfing between Hawaiian Islands or paddling the English Channel, he spends time at home with his athlete/model wife Gabrielle Reece, and their children.

tim mckenna

New York Strip Steak with Vegetables

Recipe serves 2.

ingredients

2 New York strip steaks/boneless sirloin steaks

1 carrot

1 small red onion

1 zucchini

1 red capsicum/bell pepper

Olive oil

Salt and pepper to taste

method

• Get steak out of refrigerator one hour prior to cooking.

• Slice vegetables lengthwise. Brush with oil and grill/ BBQ until cooked.

• Rub steak with oil, salt and fresh cracked pepper.

• The surface of your grill or BBQ should be clean and oiled to avoid the steak sticking.

• For best results the temperature should be hot,(you know the temperature is right when you can only hold your hand over the grill for 3-4 seconds without it being uncomfortable). Make sure you avoid piercing the steak, as this will cause the juices to be released.

• Cook steak for 4-5 minutes on each side.

• If you would like grill marks on your steak turn it 90 degrees half way through cooking.

• Serve on a large plate with vegetables. Enjoy.

Gary Elkerton

Gary Elkerton is a prime example of a power surfer. He earned the nickname "Kong" for his competitive prowess, hilarious antics, explosive free surfing and forceful style. Elkerton's professional career spanned fourteen years with numerous victories, including two wins of the prestigious Triple Crown of Surfing.

Elkerton had a unique upbringing on Australia's East Coast. He helped his father on a prawn trawler at night and had correspondence lessons by day. After discovering surfing in his early teenage years, Elkerton came to the attention of the surfing world with amazing performances in junior competitions. After an amateur career that included Queensland and Australian titles, Kong joined the professional ranks full time in 1984.

Although a standout whenever the waves were over six feet, Elkerton proved he could do it all by winning events in dismal conditions. He almost won the World Title on three separate occasions, finishing the year in second by the narrowest of margins. In the powerful surf of Hawaii's North Shore Kong proved extraordinary, executing manoeuvres few could match.

After his retirement in 1998, Kong won World Masters titles in 2000, 2001 and 2003. Today Elkerton lives with his family on Australia's East Coast and runs a swim school for children. He remains an amazing surfer and one of the sports most infamous personalities.

Chicken Tofu Stir-fry

This nutritious meal serves 4 and is relatively easy to master!

ingredients

1 red capsicum/bell pepper

1 carrot

1 red onion

½ cup of sliced mushrooms

1 floret of broccoli

1 handful of snow peas

1 bunch of coriander/cilantro

4 cloves of garlic

Ginger peeled and grated to taste

2 chicken breasts

200g (7 oz) of tofu

3 tablespoons of olive oil

4 cups of cooked brown rice

method

- Cook brown rice (see Gerry Lopez).
- Wash and slice all vegetables into bite sized pieces.
- Crush garlic and chop coriander finely.
- Dice chicken and tofu into medium pieces.
- Heat oil in a large pan or wok.
- Add garlic and ginger. Sauté for approximately 2 minutes.
- Add chicken breasts and tofu.
- Stir-fry until chicken is cooked through and tofu is golden brown.
- Remove chicken and tofu from pan and set aside.
- Add a touch more oil if needed and stir fry the vegetables until cooked.
- Add chicken and tofu back into pan with vegetables. Mix together.
- Serve on a bed of cooked brown rice.

Bruce Irons

brian bielmann

Bruce Irons ability in the water is nothing short of astounding. He enthralled the surfing world with his unearthly talent long before he joined the elite World Championship Tour. Irons innovative aerial manoeuvres, expert tube riding and superb performances in huge waves place him at the forefront of progressive surfing for the next generation.

Bruce grew up on the beautiful Hawaiian island of Kauai, a tropical paradise seeped in surf culture. He began riding waves with his older brother Andy, both boys proved competitively successful. Today Andy and Bruce are two of the best surfers in the world, however they have not forgotten their roots and every year give back to their community by holding a junior event called the Irons Brothers Pine Trees Classic.

Although Bruce is revered for his amazing free surfing ability he has won several events in a variety of conditions, a testament to his talent. In 2001 Irons became The Pipeline Masters Champion. In 2004 Bruce was named ASP Rookie of the Year and earned a place in history by winning the prestigious Eddie Aikau Big Wave Invitational at enormous Waimea Bay. Presently Bruce lives on Kauai with his family and continues to blow minds with his surfing genius.

brian bielmann

Fish Tacos with Mango Salsa

gutter photos

Recipe serves 2.

ingredients

500g (1 lb) of fish (tuna preferably)

1 ripe mango

1 small red onion

4 tablespoons of chopped coriander/cilantro

1 lime

2 tablespoons of taco seasoning

6 corn tortillas

1 tablespoon of oil

½ an iceburg lettuce

method

- Heat oven to 180°C (350°F). Wrap tortillas in foil and bake until warmed through.
- Chop mango, onion and coriander. Combine. Squeeze lime juice over mix. Set aside.
- Wash and shred lettuce.
- Dice tuna into medium sized pieces.
- In a large frying pan heat oil to medium-high.
- Add tuna and sauté quickly.
- When almost done mix in seasoning for the last minute of cooking.
- Serve tuna in tortillas with lettuce and mango salsa.

Peter Townend

tom servais

Peter Townend (PT) was the first ASP World Champion. He was a prime mover in the professionalisation of surfing, which resulted in the creation of the ASP World Tour.

Raised on Australia's Gold Coast with Rabbit Bartholomew and Michael Peterson as sparring partners, PT developed his signature style on the points of Coolangatta. Between 1976 and '79 PT was a dominant figure on the professional surfing scene, consistently ranking in the world's top five.

Townend's careful cultivation of his image made him a fixture in the surfing media. PT co-created a professional surfing team, The Bronzed Aussies, with two friends. Together they endeavored to change the representation of professional surfing. Townend was featured in many surf films including *Fantasea, Big Wednesday* and *Bustin' Down the Door*.

Since his retirement from competition PT has written extensively for a variety of publications, spent a decade plus in publishing, coached the US National Surf Team and worked with various surf wear brands. He has received many accolades including inductions into the Australia Sporting Hall of Fame and the Surfing Walk of Fame. PT has three children and resides in California, where he heads his own consultancy firm, The ActivEmpire. His favorite food is his friend Leila's following Brazilian infused dish. This is a complete meal and will easily feed a couple of starving surfers!

peter crawford

Brazilian Sausages, Rice and Veggies

twaddlebean

ingredients

6 sausages (any type of meat can be used)

2 onions

1 tomato

3 tablespoons of olive oil

1 tablespoon of vinegar

Salt and pepper to taste

4 garlic cloves

1 carrot

1 cup of brown rice

2 cups of water

1 broccoli floret

6 asparagus

100g (3.5 oz) baby spinach

method

- *Rice dish:* Cut one onion, carrot and two cloves of garlic into small pieces.
- In a saucepan heat 1 tablespoon of olive oil to medium temperature, add garlic, onion and carrot. Cook till onion slightly browns. Add washed rice and mix.
- Cover rice with water. Bring to boil, stir then cover and turn down stove to lowest setting until water absorbs.
- *Sausage dish:* Cut sausages into bite sized pieces.
- Heat 1 tablespoon of oil in frying pan to medium-high. Fry sausages for 2-3 minutes.
- Chop onion and tomato into medium pieces. Add to sausages along with vinegar.
- Cook until tender, approximately 7-10 minutes.
- *Vegetable dish*: Wash and cut broccoli and asparagus into bite sized pieces.
- Chop remaining 2 garlic cloves finely.
- Heat another frying pan to medium, add 1 tablespoon of olive oil, garlic and any of your favourite herbs. Mix in broccoli, asparagus and spinach. Cook until vegetables are warm.
- Serve sausages on a bed of rice with vegetables on the side. Season with salt and pepper.

Paige Hareb

steve dickinson/curl magazine

Paige Hareb is the reigning queen of New Zealand surfing. In 2008 Paige entered the history books as the first female surfer from her country to qualify for the ASP World Championship Tour.

From the moment her Dad pushed her into her first wave on his longboard Paige was hooked. Growing up in picturesque Taranaki on NZ's North Island gave Paige the opportunity to explore her skills in a variety of sports. Proving a talented athlete on land as well as the ocean, Paige was a member of the Wanaka Ski Academy and played soccer at a national level. However, in her early teens surfing became Paige's priority.

Hareb dominated local and national surfing contests racking up consistent results before graduating to the ultra competitive Pro Junior Circuit. With multiple wins the talented goofy footer managed to impress an international audience, attracting the attention of major sponsors.

Despite still being a teenager Paige is proving she belongs among the worlds best by consistently placing well on the WCT. With the support of not only her family but an entire nation, Paige's dream of becoming a world champion surfer may soon become a reality. The recipe Paige has chosen to share is her family's favourite Baked Fish in Curry Sauce.

steve dickinson/curl magazine

Baked Fish in Curry Sauce

Serves 4-6

ingredients

6 medium white fish fillets

1 large or 2 small sweet potatoes/yams

1 onion

2 cloves of garlic

2-3 bananas

2x 375ml (13 oz) tins of coconut cream

1 tablespoon of butter

3 tablespoons of curry powder

1 teaspoon of tumeric

1 teaspoon of mixed dried herbs

Salt and pepper to taste

method

- Preheat oven to 180°C (350°F).
- Peel sweet potato, slice into 2-3cm (1 in) rounds. Boil till cooked. Drain and set aside.
- Chop onion and garlic. Fry in butter on low heat for 5 minutes.
- Add coconut cream, stir well and bring to the boil.
- Add curry powder, tumeric, salt, pepper and dried herbs.
- Simmer for 5 minutes.
- Wash the fish, slice into cubes and add to sauce. Place in oven proof dish.
- Top with sweet potato and sliced banana. Bake for 15-20 minutes.
- Serve with rice, pasta or salad.

Mark Occhilupo

Mark Occhilupo (Occy) is a World Champion and Australian icon. The comeback king is renowned throughout the surfing world for his powerful style, backhand attack and unmistakable laugh.

Raised on the beaches of southern Sydney, Occy became a professional surfer at just sixteen. The super talented goofy footer, known as "The Raging Bull" for his raw strength, won the 1985 Pipeline Masters and the coveted OP pro twice. However, in 1988 he faded into obscurity, all but disappearing from professional surfing.

Occy admirably sought to overcome his personal demons and in 1995 made one of the most celebrated comebacks in surfing's history. It took Occy only two years to again become one of the worlds best competitive surfers. In 1997 he was ranked number two behind the legendary Kelly Slater. However it was in 1999 that Occy achieved his lifetime dream of becoming the ASP World Surfing Champion.

In 2005 after an illustrious and dramatic career spanning more than two decades, Occhilupo retired from professional surfing. The father of three presently resides on Australia's Gold Coast with his family. As Mark's wife, Mae, is Filipino, they have elected to include this delicious traditional stew recipe.

Chicken Afritada

Serves 4-6.

ingredients

1kg (2.2 lbs) of chicken thighs

6 large tomatoes

1 onion

3 cloves of garlic

3 medium potatoes

2 carrots

1 red capsicum/bell pepper

1 green capsicum/bell pepper

4 cups of water

1 chicken stock cube

¼ cup of vegetable oil

1 bay leaf

method

• Chop chicken and vegetables into bite sized pieces.

• Heat oil in a large pot.

• Sauté garlic and onion for 5 minutes.

• Add chicken and cook until chicken browns slightly.

• Add tomatoes and cook, stirring for two minutes.

• Add water, bay leaf and stock cube. Bring to boil.

• Turn heat to low, cover pot and let simmer until chicken is tender (about 15 minutes).

• Add potatoes, carrots and capsicum.

• Simmer until all vegetables are soft (about 20 minutes).

• Remove bay leaf, garnish with fresh parsley and serve with crusty bread.

Beau Young

Beau Young is a two time World Champion longboarder, professional free surfer and successful musician. The multi-talented Young does not limit his style to one genre of surfing or music.

Beau, the son of five time world champion Nat Young, grew up in Sydney's Northern Beaches with a great respect and love for the ocean. Beau rode short boards exclusively during his formative years and enjoyed a successful junior career. For a time, Young competed on the WQS but began to get disillusioned with competition. At the age of twenty one he tried a longboard, which resulted in a change of attitude and an appreciation for riding waves in different ways.

Beau developed a longboarding style that encompassed both traditional and progressive elements. This combination proved successful and resulted in Beau winning two World Titles in 2000 and 2003. After his second world title, at the peak of his career, Beau announced his retirement from competitive surfing to focus on his musical endeavours. His subsequent albums, *Waves of Change* and *One Step at a Time* have enjoyed international success. Presently Beau lives in rural Byron Bay where he surfs daily on a variety of boards. He is living the dream, expressing his creativity as a professional free surfer and touring musician.

Layered Tuna Pie

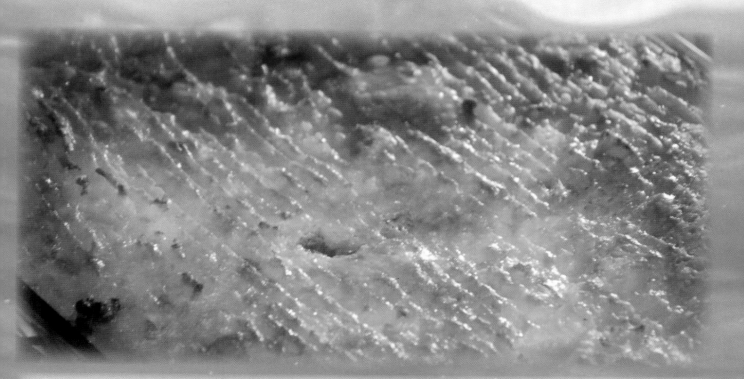

This is a warm and hearty meal perfect for winter nights. Serves 6-8.

ingredients

1 onion

1 capsicum/bell pepper

3 stalks of celery

4 tablespoons of butter

2 tablespoons of flour

500ml (16 oz) of milk

1 x 420g (15 oz) can of tinned tuna in brine

1 x 420g (15 oz) can of tinned peas

1 x 420g (15 oz) can of creamed corn

2 potatoes

½ a medium pumpkin/butternut squash

1 cup of grated cheddar cheese

Season with salt and pepper

method

- Preheat oven to 180°C (350°F).
- *First Layer:* Finely chop onion, capsicum and celery. Fry in 1 tablespoon of butter until tender.
- Make well in centre of fried vegetables and add 2 additional tablespoons of butter and flour. Stir. Add milk and drained tuna. Stir until smooth and thickened.
- Place in bottom of large casserole dish.
- *Second Layer:* Mix together peas and creamed corn.
- Place in casserole dish on top of the 1st layer.
- *Third Layer:* Peel and roughly chop potato and pumpkin, boil until cooked. Drain and mash.
- Mix in 1 tablespoon of butter and season with salt and pepper.
- Spread on top of second layer. Sprinkle with grated cheese.
- Bake for 30 minutes or until golden brown.
- Serve with side salad and crusty bread.

Jordy Smith

swilly.com

Jordy Smith is a sensational surfer. A free surfing phenomenon, Smith manages to translate his brilliance into contest results regardless of the conditions. Undoubtedly Jordy has the talent, drive and competitive nous necessary to reach the pinnacle of his sport.

Introduced to surfing at a young age by his father, Jordy developed his trademark flair amongst the waves of Durban, South Africa. His unmistakable talent gained recognition and saw him win ten South African National Titles. Also athletic on land, as a junior Jordy was asked to play for the National Soccer Team.

In 2006 Jordy won the ASP World Junior Championship and the Vans Triple Crown Rookie of the Year award. 2007 saw Jordy take on the gruelling World Qualifying Series. Remarkably he not only qualified for the Dream Tour, but won the WQS by a record margin.

What sets Smith apart from other wave riders is his combination of aerial surfing, power and fluidity. Fast, innovative and always exciting to watch, Jordy's profile in and out of the water continues to rise. The following chicken dish is one of his favourites and has been graciously submitted by Jordy's Mum, Luellen.

swilly.com

Chicken a la Lulu

gutter photos

This recipe is easy and delicious. Serves 4.

ingredients

4-6 chicken breast fillets

1 onion

1 capsicum/green pepper

1 punnet of button mushrooms

1 x 400g (14 oz) tub of cream

1 packet of brown onion soup

2 cloves garlic or garlic flakes

Salt and black pepper to taste

method

- Dice chicken and slice all vegetables.
- Heat oil in electric frying pan.
- Add onion and garlic cook until nicely browned.
- Add capsicum and mushrooms. Stir.
- Add chopped chicken and gently stir all ingredients together until almost done.
- Add brown onion soup powder and cream
- Stir gently until soup and cream have mixed nicely into the other ingredients.
- May add milk if sauce is too thick.
- Allow to simmer for a few minutes.
- Serve on a bed of rice with a side salad.

desserts

Pam Burridge

tom servais

Pam Burridge is one of Australia's most successful female surfers. Winning twenty ASP professional events and the 1990 World Title, Pam's career spanned over nineteen years.

Burridge grew up in an athletic family in Sydney, Australia. At ten, Pam began surfing at the famous Manly Beach on a homemade board. She started entering contests soon after, often taking on the boys due to a lack of female opponents.

Amazingly, Burridge turned professional at the tender age of fifteen and experienced immediate success. Over the next fifteen years Burridge would consistently be ranked among the worlds best.

Due to her natural athleticism, raw talent and smooth style, Burridge had the expectations of an entire nation upon her to bring home Australia's first ASP Female World Title. Pam overcame numerous obstacles to eventually win the 1990 World Championship in pumping surf at Hawaii's Sunset Beach.

Burridge retired from the circuit in 1999. She lives with her family in Bendalong NSW where she and her shaper husband, Mark Rabbidge, run a surf school and two successful surfboard companies, including the female orientated brand, Feisty Girl.

tom servais

Orange Poppy Seed Cake

gutter photos

Pam has kindly shared her luscious orange poppy seed cake recipe. Perfect served with a dollop of thick cream and a cup of tea.

ingredients

Cake

½ cup of poppy seeds

½ cup of yoghurt

200g (7 oz) of butter

1 tablespoon of finely grated orange rind

1 cup of caster sugar

3 eggs

1 ½ cups of sifted self raising flour (or 1 ½ cups of all purpose flour plus 2 teaspoons of baking powder)

½ cup of sifted plain flour

½ cup of almond meal

¾ cup of fresh orange juice

Syrup

2 cups of caster sugar

1 cup of fresh orange juice

1 cup of water

½ cup of grated orange rind

method

- *Cake*: Preheat oven to 180°C (350°F). Grease and line cake tin.
- Combine poppy seeds and yoghurt. Set aside.
- Place butter, orange rind and sugar in a bowl. Beat until light and creamy. Add eggs and mix.
- Stir through poppy seed mix, flours, almond meal and orange juice.
- Transfer mix to cake tin. Bake for 50 minutes.
- *Syrup*: Stir sugar, orange juice, rind and water over medium heat until sugar dissolves.
- Simmer until slightly thickened.
- Pour half the hot syrup over warm cake. Serve the rest over each individual slice.

Andy Irons

brian biemann

Andy Irons is a three time world champion and one of the dominant competitors of the new millennium. His unique combination of versatility and competitive drive has culminated in numerous WCT victories and captured fans worldwide.

Irons was born on the idyllic tropical island of Kauai to surfing parents. He began riding waves at age eight with his younger brother Bruce. Both boys went on to have multiple junior wins and climbed the competitive ladder together.

Andy turned pro in 1996 and joined the elite WCT in 1998. Irons had solid finishes on tour between 1998 and 2001 but really came into his own in 2002 when he won the prestigious Pipeline Masters, Triple Crown and ASP World Title. It was the ultimate trifecta, which historically Irons managed to replicate in 2003 during an intense nail biting Pipeline Masters final against Kelly Slater. In 2004 he convincingly won the world title for a third year without being seriously challenged by any other competitor.

Irons has been featured in numerous surf films notably *Campaign 2, Raw Irons* and *Trilogy*. Presently Andy lives in Hawaii with his wife Lyndie and continues to impress fans the world over with his exciting competitive act and mind blowing free surfing.

swilly.com

Chocolate Brownie Supreme

This amazing brownie recipe is simply delicious. It can be eaten as a snack or dressed up into a scrumptious dessert.

ingredients

150g (5 oz) of butter

300g (10 oz) of dark chocolate

½ cup of brown sugar

¼ cup of raw sugar

3 eggs lightly beaten

1½ cups of plain flour

1 cup of white chocolate chips

500ml (1 pint) of vanilla ice cream

Chocolate syrup

⅓ cup of Kahlua

1 packet of slivered almonds

1 punnet of fresh raspberries

method

• Preheat oven to 180°C (350°F).
• Combine butter and chocolate in heat proof bowl over saucepan full of simmering water. Be careful not to let the bowl's bottom touch the water.
• When melted remove from heat. Add sugar, eggs, flour and lastly chocolate chips.
• Mix till combined.
• Grease and line brownie/biscuit tin. Pour in mix and cook for 35-40 minutes.
• Allow to cool then cut brownies into squares.
• Do the following for a fancy dessert: drizzle chocolate sauce on a plate. Soak the bottom of each brownie in kahlua and place on top of chocolate sauce. Top with a scoop of ice cream. Sprinkle with almonds and fresh raspberries.

Mark Richards

tom servais

Mark Richards (MR) is one of the greatest surfers of all time. A four time consecutive World Champion and renowned shaper, Richards has earned his place as one of surfing's most respected legends.

Richards began surfing at just six years old. His father Ray, owned one of Australia's first surf shops in Newcastle. After a successful junior career, MR decided to leave school and pursue professional surfing. He proved himself immediately with a fantastic showing at enormous Waimea Bay. In addition to competing, Richards shaped surfboards under the tutelage of Dick Brewer.

During his World Title years from 1979-1982, Richards was completely dominant. One of the crucial elements of MR's supremacy was his modification of the twin fin surfboard design, which he refashioned to suit his style and size. The result was a board that proved fantastic in the World Tour conditions.

Richards has been featured in countless articles, movies and has won almost every accolade in surfing. Both easygoing and humble, MR is undoubtedly one of surfing's nicest characters. Presently Mark lives in Newcastle with his family where he continues to surf, shape and run his successful shop. Mark's favourite snacks are rock cakes made by his wife Jenny.

tom servais

Rock Cakes

Recipe makes 12-15 biscuits.

ingredients
2 cups of organic self raising flour

¾ cup of sugar

1 teaspoon of mixed spice

90g (3 oz) of unsalted butter

1 cup of dried fruit (sultanas, currants &
chopped apricots)

1 egg (preferably free-range)

½ cup of milk

method
• Preheat oven to 180°C (350°F).
• Put the dry ingredients in the bowl of a food processor. If you don't have a food
  processor just mix by hand in a large bowl.
• Add the butter and mix.
• Add dried fruit.
• Then add egg and milk. Mix until just combined.
• Spoon onto a greased tray and bake for 15-20 minutes.

Bryce Young

Bryce Young is an extremely multi-talented surfer. Amazing on both short and longboards, Bryce could do either professionally. In 2008 at the age of seventeen Bryce was ranked number fifteen on the World Longboard Tour and continues to impress with his short board repertoire.

Bryce grew up amongst the incredible waves of Angourie on Australia's East Coast. The youngest son of world champion, Nat, Bryce began surfing tandem with his Dad at the age of three. He switched to his own board at five and hasn't looked back. He began competing at the age of eleven and has had numerous wins on both long and short boards, including the Noosa Festival of Surfing.

Young not only rides waves but also snowboards and skates. His talent on different boards and mediums has undoubtedly contributed to his accomplishments. Although a successful competitor, Bryce simply loves the freedom and creative expression that surfing allows him. Young travels constantly for competitions and photo shoots but still calls Angourie home. His favourite food is his Mum, Ti's Banana Cake, which she has kindly shared.

swilly.com

Angourie Banana Cake

gutter photos

This cake is easy and quick to make. It is prepared in one bowl and does not require any complicated steps. Mixture can also be put into muffin tins and makes approximately 16 muffins. Reduce cooking time to 15-20 minutes.

ingredients

125g (4.5 oz) of butter

1 cup of raw sugar

1 teaspoon of bi-carb or baking soda

3-4 large ripe bananas

2 cups of self raising flour (or 2 cups of all purpose flour plus 3 teaspoons of baking powder)

1 cup of milk (soy milk can be substituted)

2 teaspoons of vanilla essence

Cream Cheese Icing

125g (4.5 oz) of cream cheese

2 cups of icing sugar

1 teaspoon of vanilla essence

2 tablespoons of liquid (can be lemon juice, melted butter or water)

method

- *Cake:* Preheat oven to 180°C (350°F).
- Melt butter in a large bowl in microwave. Add sugar and stir with wooden spoon.
- Mash bananas, then add to mix along with bi-carb soda. Stir.
- Stir in flour. Add milk and vanilla. Mix again with spoon until combined.
- Pour into greased cake tin and cook for 35 minutes or until skewer inserted comes out clean.
- *Icing:* Beat all ingredients together with an electric mixer until smooth.
- Spread evenly over cooled cake and serve. This icing is creamy and rich. It makes the banana cake even more delicious!

Lynne Boyer

Lynne Boyer is a two time World Champion and renowned artist. During the '70s Lynne helped push the boundaries of female, high performance surfing.

Boyer was born in Allentown, Pennsylvania in 1956. After catching her first wave atop a surf mat on the New Jersey shore she was hooked. She began surfing in earnest at eleven when her family moved to the tropical paradise of Hawaii.

Lynne amazed the judges of women's surfing throughout the '70s and '80s, winning two consecutive world titles and four World Cup of Surfing Crowns before leaving the competitive scene in 1984. Known for her radical style and intense rivalry with Margo Oberg, Lynne is credited with bringing women's surfing to a new level. She has been inducted into the Surfing Walk of Fame and the Hawaii Sports Hall of Fame.

Today Lynne resides in Hawaii with her partner, where she works on her various art projects. Her involvement with the ocean gives her a unique perspective on her surroundings, which is the focus of her work.

LB's Chocolate Chip Cookies

These cookies are amazingly good and will disappear before your very eyes.

ingredients

½ cup or 115g (4 oz) of unsalted butter
½ cup of brown sugar
¼ cup of white sugar
2 teaspoons of vanilla extract
1 large egg
¼ teaspoon of salt

½ teaspoon of bi-carb soda/baking soda
1⅛ cups of plain flour
1½ cups of good quality chocolate chips
½ cup of nuts cut in halves (roasted hazelnuts, macadamias or pecans)

method

- Preheat oven to 190°C (375°F).
- Mix together butter, sugars, vanilla, egg and salt in a large bowl.
- Then add soda and flour. Mix till combined.
- Add the chocolate and nuts (Lynne's tip is to add heaps of goodies, the dough should just hold all the chocolate and nuts together).
- Place spoonfuls of dough on lined cookie tray.
- Bake in oven for 8-12 minutes.

Romain Maurin

Romain Maurin is one of France's best surfers. A two time European champion, Romain has been ranked among longboarding's best for over a decade.

Born in the tropical paradise of French Polynesia, Maurin's parents moved to France's Basque region when he was just six years old. Romain's father is legendary French surfer Francois-Xavier Maurin. A multiple national champion FX, as he is known, was a top ranked professional longboard surfer in the 1980s.

It is no wonder, with his fathers' influence, that Romain chose to pursue his surfing dream on a longboard. With skills honed on the abundant waves of the Basque Coast, Romain developed his trademark style. Maurin's unique mix of traditional and progressive maneuvers set him apart from other surfers. Just as comfortable hanging ten as he is hitting the lip, Romain quickly climbed longboarding's competitive ranks.

Considered among the world's best for over ten years Romain continues to compete at an international level. Featured in numerous articles, books and surf films, Maurin lives in France where he studies podiatry. Romain's mother, Dominique, is an amazing cook and has generously shared her scrumptious warm apple cake.

Apple Cake

twaddle bean

This recipe is quick, easy and amazingly good.

ingredients

1kg (2.2 lbs or approximately 6) apples

Caramel

4 tablespoons of brown sugar

2 tablespoons of water

Topping

5 tablespoons of brown sugar

2 eggs

100g (3.5 oz) of softened butter

4 tablespoons of plain flour

1 teaspoon of yeast

method

- *Caramel:* In a microwaves safe dish approximately 20-25cm (8-10 in) in diameter, mix together sugar and water. Cook in microwave for 6 minutes until it starts to turn brown.
- Peel and thinly slice apples. Place apples evenly over the caramel.
- *Topping:* In a medium bowl mix together all topping ingredients.
- Spread mixture evenly over the apples.
- Cook in microwave for 12 minutes on high.
- Serve cake warm with vanilla ice cream or custard.

Mark Warren

robbi newman

Mark Warren was one of the most successful and charismatic professional surfers of the 1970s. Always a gentleman and dedicated supporter of professional surfing, Mark has worked within the surfing industry for over three decades.

Mark started surfing at age eleven on Sydney's Northern Beaches. His talent was instantly recognisable and earned him numerous junior titles. In 1976 Warren won the Australian National Title and competed in the first World Circuit Tour. Always a standout regardless of the conditions, Mark won the Hawaiian Smirnoff Pro and finished the year rated number four. A founding member of the Bronzed Aussies, Warren had his best professional results in large waves winning the esteemed Duke Classic in 1980.

After his retirement from professional surfing, Mark worked extensively in the media as a presenter, radio host and writer. His critically acclaimed book, *The Atlas of Australian Surfing*, has enjoyed several editions.

Warren has also remained closely connected with the surfing community. He has acted as a tour representative, contest commentator, junior coach and presently works for surf wear giant Quiksilver. A 2007 inductee into the Australian Surfing Hall of Fame, Mark resides in Sydney with his wife Helen and children Max and Holly. He still rides waves whenever he can.

peter crawford

Anzac Biscuits

twaddlebean

Originally made as a nutritious supplement for Australian WWI soldiers by their loved ones. Anzac biscuits, as they became known after Gallipoli, are seeped in tradition and enjoyed by Australians of all ages. Recipe makes approximately 15 biscuits.

ingredients

125g (4.5 oz) of butter

1 tablespoon of golden syrup

2 tablespoons of water

½ teaspoon of bi-carb or baking soda

1 cup of rolled oats

1 cup of shredded coconut

1 cup of plain flour

¾ cup of sugar

method

• Preheat oven to 170°C (340°F). Grease and line biscuit tray.

• Melt butter, golden syrup, water and soda together in a saucepan.

• In a large bowl combine oats, coconut, flour and sugar.

• Pour butter mixture into dry ingredients and mix until combined.

• Roll mixture into medium sized balls and arrange on tray.

• Bake for approximately 15 minutes or until golden brown.

• Cool on wire rack and enjoy.

Stephanie Gilmore

Stephanie Gilmore is at the forefront of progressive surfing. One of the most talked about athletes in women's sport, her fluidity, power and style are world renowned. In 2007, Steph's first year on the World Circuit Tour, she was both ASP World Champion and rookie of the year- a remarkable feat. In 2008 she backed it up, becoming World Champion two years running.

Gilmore grew up on Australia's East Coast and began surfing as a child. She had remarkable success as a junior where her talent was first recognized. As a teenager, before turning professional, she won two elite WCT events. She is the only person in history to do so.

Her remarkable talent, easygoing attitude and huge smile have seen Steph win a worldwide fan base and earn the nickname, "Happy Gilmore". Her potential seems boundless and is only enhanced by her personality. Undoubtedly Steph is a fantastic ambassador for women's surfing; we can rest assured that the future is in good hands! Steph has chosen to include her Mum's fruit cake recipe which is a fantastic snack perfect for afternoon tea.

Boiled Fruit Cake

ingredients

1 cup of caster sugar

1 cup of cold water

185g (6.5 oz) of butter

1 teaspoon of bi-carb or baking soda

1 teaspoon of ground dried ginger

1 teaspoon of cinnamon

1 teaspoon of nutmeg

2 cups of sultanas or other dried fruits/nuts

2 eggs

1 cup of plain flour

1 cup of self raising flour (or 1 cup of all purpose flour plus 1½ teaspoons of baking powder)

¼ cup of orange juice

¼ cup of brandy or other liquor of your choice

method

• Preheat oven to 160°C (320°F).
• Grease and line approximately 25cm (10 in) diameter round cake pan.
• Place sugar, water, butter, ginger, cinnamon, nutmeg and sultanas (or substitute) in a pot on low heat.
• Once butter is melted and sugar is dissolved, add bi-carb soda and simmer for 10 minutes.
• Turn off heat and cool.
• Once cooled add lightly beaten eggs and flours to the pot. Fold till combined.
• Mix in orange juice.
• Pour into prepared tin and bake for approximately an hour and a half or until golden brown.
• While still warm, pour liquor evenly over cake.

Eduardo Bagé

Eduardo Bagé is an extremely talented surfer. Consistently ranking among the top longboarders in the world, he spends his time between his homes in Brazil and France.

Growing up in Rio de Janeiro, Bagé began surfing before he could swim. At the tender age of seven Eduardo took to the waves in front of his house on a polystyrene board. However it would take fifteen years until he fell in love with longboarding. He hasn't stopped since.

After entering his first longboard competition in 1996, Bagé has had numerous wins including the Rio Pro Brazil in 2007 and the 2006 Festival Petrobras. His combination of traditional and radical manoeuvres has seen him carve a name for himself in the surfing community. In the 2008 World Longboard Tour Bagé posted his best results to date ranking fifth overall by the years end.

Due to his military training and extensive travels, Bagé speaks French, English, Spanish and Portuguese fluently. He and his wife, Audrey, also a surfer, are kept busy with their two young sons and a life spanning two continents. One of his favorite taste combinations is banana and chocolate.

Chocolate Stuffed Bananas

gutter photos

This recipe is ridiculously simple but tastes fantastic. It can be baked in the oven, barbequed or thrown in a fire.

ingredients
4 large bananas
115g (4 oz) of chocolate. Can be any type but dark tastes best.
Vanilla ice cream to serve

method
- Chop chocolate into small pieces.
- Leaving the skin on, slice the banana lengthways. Be careful not to cut the banana all the way through, you are just making a pocked for the chocolate.
- Scoop out approximately 1 tablespoons of flesh from each banana. Again be careful not to pierce the skin.
- Stuff the bananas evenly with the chocolate.
- Wrap each banana individually in foil and bake/BBQ for about 10 minutes or until the chocolate is melted.
- Serve with vanilla ice cream. It is even delicious simply scooped out of the skin with a spoon. Enjoy!

Peter "Pan" Panagiotis

Peter Pan is an American surfing icon. The East Coast legend has owned shops, surf schools and won countless competitions.

Born Peter Panagiotis, "Pan" as he is widely known, began surfing at age thirteen in Rhode Island. The energetic natural-footer started entering competitions in 1967 and has over a hundred regional titles to his credit in numerous divisions. Not content to limit his enjoyment of the ocean to one piece of equipment, Pan longboards, shortboards, bodysurfs, kneeboards and stand up paddles.

A member of the East Coast Surfing Hall of Fame, Pan is active in organizing and directing events for organisations such as the National Association of Surf Schools and Instructors. The Peter Pan Surf School has been in operation for over 30 years and introduced thousands of people to the ocean. His signature 'Slug' model surfboard has been one of Hobie's best sellers for decades.

The perpetually stoked Pan never passes up an opportunity to get in the water. From two inches to ten feet, sun, sleet or snow he's out there. It's both refreshing and inspiring to see. As Peter is of Greek decent, he has chosen to contribute this traditional recipe.

Kourabiethes

These Greek almond treats are delicious. Serve with a good strong cup of coffee.

ingredients

175g (6 oz) of butter

⅓ cup of olive oil

⅛ cup of sugar

1 beaten egg

¼ teaspoon of bi-carb or baking soda

2 teaspoons of cognac or brandy

2 cups of almond meal

¼ teaspoon of cinnamon

2¼ cups of plain flour

1 cup of icing sugar

method

• Preheat oven to 180°C (350°F). Place baking paper on two large biscuit trays.
• In a large bowl beat together butter, sugar and olive oil till light and fluffy. Note this is much easier with an electric mixer.
• Stir in egg, soda, brandy, cinnamon and almonds.
• Stir in flour gradually then knead on a flat surface until dough is a large ball.
• Form pieces of the dough into balls roughly the size of walnuts and place onto the baking tray.
• Bake in oven for 15-20 minutes.
• When they are slightly cool, coat each ball in icing sugar.

Acknowledgements

First of all, a huge thank you to the surfers for sharing their favourite foods and recipes. I am extremely grateful to all of them for taking a chance and being involved in such a different type of book.

Thank you, to the contributing photographers who kindly provided me with such remarkable shots.

To the lovely Jenny and Simon Williams my amazing friends, who are so generous with their photographs and time.

Thanks to Meiki T for her designing brilliance and John Witzig for giving me guidance. Another big thank you to Chris Nicoll for being such a great editor and wading through hundreds of pages!

Personally this book would never have been finished, or even started, without the help and encouragement of my beautiful family. They have been cooking, eating, researching, reading, photographing, shopping and supporting me every step of the way. So to Mum, Dad, Bryce and Taylor thank you from the bottom of my heart.

tj taylor bryce tully travis